ROOFTOP ARCHITECTURE

Rooftop
Architecture
Building on an
elevated surface

Ed Melet / Eric Vreedenburgh

NAi Publishers

Contents

Superstudio,

Life-supersurface-spring

cleaning,

1971

Preface

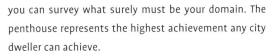

Hey (hey) you (you), get off of my cloud, two's a crowd...
(Mick Jagger, '99th Floor)

In the city, the penthouse is the place to be. It is close to heaven, far above the din and smells of the city. There is nobody above you, meaning that you are king of the mountain. Elevated above the masses,

you can survey what surely must be your domain. The penthouse represents the highest achievement any city dweller can achieve.

It was not always so. For centuries, the high point in a residential structure was a place either to stow away the servants under the eaves, or to stand watch over a landscape filled with danger. Then, the piano nobile was the place to be: above the garbage and the commerce of the street, but not too far away from its culture to lose touch and, above all else, not too high up to be inconvenient.

What elevated this preferred position was the lift, which made getting to the top of a building just as easy as staying at the bottom. Yet it was not just a mechanical invention that suddenly opened up the upper floors to speculation and spectacular views. The very notion that one could survey and thus visually control the environment was born in the democratization of the visual realm in early-18th-century Paris and London. If at one time only the king could sit high in his palace or opera box and see the world as he had made it and as it should be, now the new middle-class citizens could rise up in a balloon, in structures such as the Eiffel Tower, or in the virtual promontory of the panorama. There, they could take control of all they could see, if only for a moment and only through the knowledge a view provides.

Translating that fashion into a desire to live high up in a building took some time. The impulse was strengthened by such cultural phenomena as the artist's studio, originally located in the attic because that was were rents were cheapest and the light was best, but later seen as the model of a free zone in the new metropolis where, – not by coincidence – vision reigned supreme. Vacation experiences such as at Alpine resort hotels with their views down the valleys of St Moritz and Gstaad also helped fuel the desire for a room with a view. Architects such as Le Corbusier finally brought the desire for a view of nature back into the city by promoting the notion of a free zone on top of a building, where a new kind of nature, more perfect, more abstract, and more mechanical, could replace the imperfect garden that real estate reality was squeezing out of the city.

The first penthouses of fashionable repute and inflated price appeared in New York in the Art Deco apartment buildings of the 1920s and 1930s, though examples of the type appeared almost simultaneously in the large cities of Western Europe as well. Films and novels soon turned the phenomenon into the symbol of the highest achievement and elegance. It also came to stand for a new form of division between rich and poor. Instead of isolating themselves in palaces or separate districts, a move that was in any case no longer tenable in the crowded city, the rich now kept a vertical distance from those below them. Perhaps it is for this reason that the penthouse never achieved the same aura in more socially equal countries such as those of Northern Europe.

Now the penthouse, especially in these latter countries, has taken on a new task and image. It has become an often temporary structure, placed on existing buildings as an afterthought or as the result of a renovation. It usually houses a member of the new global elite: the wandering professional, who alights in such an eyrie for a project, then flits to the next urban hot spot. It owes as much to the experience of a modern high-rise hotel as it does to the history of apartment dwellings. Rooftop Architecture, as this phenomenon is known, relies on light, modular structures that do not make too many demands on a building's infrastructure. Of course, there are more elaborate, more permanent and more socially diffuse top-ups, but the modular penthouse hut best represents the essence of the penthouse: a place of isolated, urbane culture, perched high above the city, yet part of it, that provides a home for those who are in control, even if their power is these days more and more ephemeral and invisible.

It seems as if the most desirable place of residence in the city is still moving up and becoming more and more ephemeral. Perhaps some day soon the penthouse will rise up to its apotheosis and become only a cloud, floating above the city as that urban scene itself dissolves into pure networks. Until then, we still have the penthouse from which we can survey the metropolitan scene.

Aaron Betsky

Introduction

Chic conference rooms, museums and penthouses: if something is built on the roof in Europe, Japan, Australia or North America, it is usually something unusual. Building on roofs is apparently exclusive. Perhaps that is why it has only been done on an incidental basis to date. In other parts of the world (Africa, Asia and South America) building on the roof – however skimpy it may be – is more or less normal. This is where the poorest people live. They have usurped the roof in order to be close to the economic activity. Hidden villages with accommodation of all kinds are situated on this second level. They may be homes, but also shops, small businesses, snack bars and even miniature farms.

There are several reasons to make more intensive use of the roofs in the cities of the West. The exclusiveness has to go, because the cities are growing and being eroded at the same time. They are stripping themselves of their own meanings. In the past, a relatively small and clearly identifiable area was used for housing, workplaces, shops and recreation. The city was where everything happened, surrounded by the green countryside. This conventionally layered city has been decaying for the past hundred years or so. Residents, companies, large shops and industries have left the city for a variety of reasons. Often they moved to easily accessible locations and municipalities on the outskirts of the city where there was more space and air. As a result, almost every part of the city has assumed a uniform character: exclusively residential, exclusively for work, exclusively for shopping, or exclusively for production. Naturally enough, these are extensively used areas, obliging the city to occupy more and more space, although there are fewer residents and less economic activity there than some forty years ago. Moreover, the exodus of residents and businesses confronts the city with social and economic problems. After all, only those who are able to do so go to live and/or work elsewhere. To reverse the trend, almost all major cities in the Netherlands have launched programmes to lure businesses and people with higher and middle-range incomes back to the city. Abandoned industrial estates are transformed into fashionable business and residential districts (such as the Eastern Docklands and GWL in Amsterdam, Kop van Zuid in Rotterdam, Laakhaven in The Hague, and the Sphinx Céramique site in Maastricht), and postwar housing estates are redeveloped to make them more attractive to a wider public. Every vacant spot in the city is filled. Strangely enough, most local authorities have overlooked one potential development site: the roof.

Dynamism of a city

Nature shows that complex systems have a higher chance of survival than simple ones. The health of cities also proves to be strongly correlated with the diversity that they offer in a variety of fields.

Even from an economic point of view, it is not just a matter of flexibility and diversity within the productive environment, but equally of the situation of that productive environment within a specific social context, a general climate in which the quality of housing, the cultural space and the information networks play a large role.

In this sense one could speak of the creative potential of a particular city. The same applies at other scale levels, such as institutions and businesses. 'Businesses realise that the internal development of knowledge is often insufficient to produce the innovations that they need for the longer term. In principle, innovation bears on all aspects of the running of the company. It is thus more than just technological innovation. Genuine innovations of this kind require a climate in which different disciplines and cultures can complement and reinforce one another' (Go et al., 2003).

The roof is hardly appreciated in the West. It is 'merely' the top of the building, while potentially it could be the foundation of a new layer. That is how the roof was seen in the past: many Amsterdam canal houses acquired an extra storey over the years. Besides, the flat roofs of many buildings in the Netherlands make rooftop construction a relatively simple matter.

The roof as new land for building is interesting because there is so much of it. A general, but very conservative estimate of the building potential in **The Hague** indicates that a mere 2.3 per cent of the usable flat roofs would yield an extra surface area of half a million square metres, enough for some 3,600 homes. (Buildings dating from before 1910 have not been included in this estimate because they would probably not be able to support the weight of an extra floor.)

And yet, rooftop construction is rare in the Netherlands. There are various reasons for this. Building on the roof is tricky, lightweight construction systems, which are uncommon in this country, have to be used, and access to the new layer is often a problem. All of these factors make it expensive. Moreover, owners and the present occupiers are not often keen to have building done on their roof.

Access

After construction, access to the rooftop is the largest problem. How are users to reach the roof? This often means that a new lift has to be built or the existing one extended. That is an expensive business, but a new lift will benefit the whole building. Moreover, the lift shaft is often used to give stability to the rooftop building. Besides these regular forms of access, it is of course essential to have sufficient escape routes.

Rotterdam is the only place where there is now a specific incentive policy to build a large number of penthouses in the city centre. Other cities prefer to expand horizontally rather than vertically. Horizontal expansion is easier, and may in the end be more prestigious, too. Finally, there are hardly any interesting examples of rooftop buildings in the Netherlands.

Building on the roof is still regarded as **topping up**. Prewar apartments, as well as flats from the 1950s, 1960s and 1970s, were topped up with a new layer of housing units. In social, functional and often architectural terms as well, nothing was really added to a building or a district in this way. The same target group was served. The only result was a more intensive use of the land. At the same time, topping up created negative publicity for rooftop construction. Research in Amsterdam and elsewhere revealed that it was expensive, and in many cases it was recommended to demolish the old buildings and to construct new ones. But this only applies to topping up; different rules apply to building on the roof.

Topping up

An old term for buildings on the roof, not to be confused with rooftop construction. This building practice mainly adds a lot of the same, without any differentiation in housing. The only aim was to increase volume.

One of the most important characteristics of rooftop buildings is that a new dimension is added to a building and district. In most of the rooftop buildings that have been constructed to date, it is usually an architectural contrast that has been achieved. The client accepts the disadvantages of a rooftop house or office (price, lack of a garden and of a door opening onto the street), but naturally wants something special in return. The location (near or actually in the centre) and the view can offer compensation, but the gain should primarily be sought in the architecture. Like the more expensive architectural villas, rooftop construction can become an architectural lab for which new concepts are and have to be devised. For instance, the roof offers all kinds of opportunities to experiment with flexible buildings that can be dismantled. The most natural construction systems for rooftop construction (**timber frame** or **steel frame construction**) already possess these intrinsic qualities, which make it possible to create genuinely dynamic buildings which expand or contract to meet the demands of the users.

The board room of the Schuppich Sporn & Winishofer firm of solicitors in Vienna, that of the **ING head office in Budapest**, or William Alsop's spectacular box in which the Ontario College of Arts and Design is housed, are all examples of rooftop buildings that are in principle nothing but expansions of the underlying functions. Penthouses are already a step further because they can take the shape of a social and architectural addition to a building and district. Rooftop buildings that genuinely add a new architectural, economic, functional and social dimension have not been built yet. Archipelontwerpers' redevelopment plan for the **Black Madonna**, in The Hague which included not only penthouses but also a park and an athletics track, would have offered this variety, but the building is being demolished to make way for nothing but offices.

The importance of building on the rooftop lies in the fact that the roof functions as a raised ground level on which – in theory – anything can happen, accommodating that one, specific function that the building or district requires and for which there is no space on the traditional ground level. This is one way of restoring the layered nature of the traditional city.

The final characteristic of rooftop buildings is the passion with which they are created. There is already more than enough mediocrity around, and there is no room for it on the roof. It is too unusual a location for that. If the second ground level is to succeed and to make an impact on the rest of the city, it must dazzle.

This book is a plea for rooftop construction. We are convinced that, in terms of both architecture and urban development, it is an interesting way of enriching urban environments and intensifying the use of the city. This book does not aim to offer a comprehensive picture of what has been built on roofs to date, because such a panorama is lacking at the moment. No doubt incredibly beautiful rooftop buildings have been created which we do not know about, simply because they have never been published. On the other hand, it is still too early for such an overall picture. A retrospective often charts a particular development and at the same time concludes it. Rooftop buildings, on the other hand, have not come into their own yet. Of course there are many interesting projects, but at the moment they are so incidental and scattered among different cities that there cannot be any question of their having made an impact on the city and on urban life itself.

Finally, a word on the structure of the book. Our manifesto comprises four chapters: Urban transformation, Stacking strategies, Topping up versus rooftop construction, and Building methods.

These are followed by a large number of satellite texts in which concepts that arise in the course of the manifesto are explained, either briefly and succinctly or in more breadth and depth. They place our ideas in a wider context. Readers can devise their own route through the material thanks to the layered nature of text and image. We hope that this will inspire new rooftop projects. On the other hand, reading and/or leafing through the book is a metaphor for the unpredictable and exciting rooftop landscape that we have in mind.

Ed Melet
Eric Vreedenburgh

Ferropolis brown coal mine,

Dessau

Wimmenauer, Szabo,
Kaspar and Meyer,
**City superstructure
above Dusseldorf,**
model, 1969

Rooftop construction:
a dazzling new ground level

Urban transformations

You can only allocate land once. Despite the shortage of space, we need more and more of it. The population is growing, the average number of square metres per capita is growing, and so is the number of one-person or two-person households. The economy and the infrastructure have to find ways of growing too to keep up with the demand for more, better and faster. At the same time, most people feel that the landscape – nature – should be spared as much as possible, which means that urban growth will have to take place mainly within the cities themselves.

The creation of compact cities was the objective of the Supplement to the Fourth Policy Document on Spatial Planning (1997), known as Vinex. It was an attempt to end the development that had been set in motion by the Second Policy Document (1966) – the designation of growth cores to release pressure on the congested large cities – once and for all. The development of these growth cores had led to an unprecedented building programme, with Zoetermeer, Capelle aan de IJssel and Purmerend as the best-known and most successful cities. But the downside of that success was that it was above all the richest who left the city.

Vinex enabled the large cities to tackle the competition with the growth cores by proposing that some 750,000 homes be built in and around the main cities. Since the development was in the hands of market forces, most of these homes took the form of terraced houses with (small) gardens, in line with what most Dutch people prefer. These **Vinex housing estates** were a financial success too. The houses sold like hot cakes.

However, figures issued by Statistics Netherlands in 2004 indicate that the exodus from the big cities has not stopped – it has just slowed down. In the past nine years – the Vinex heyday – the number of Dutch-born residents within the original city boundaries has fallen by almost 130,000. Once again it is those with an average or higher than average income that have abandoned the city. Their place has been taken by immigrants, who on average comprise 57 per cent of the population of the cities. The majority of these immigrants have a lower level of education and few prospects in the urban economies, which are particularly in need of highly trained workers. That is why unemployment in the cities is above the national average, and why they have benefited to a much lesser extent from the extreme economic growth of the 1990s.

Not just residents, but also businesses have turned their back on the (inner) city, a process which got under way much earlier. There were already calls during the first congresses of **CIAM** (Congrès Internationaux d'Architecture Moderne) in the late 1920s for a separation of urban functions in order to create cleaner housing areas. The first to leave was (heavy) industry. This certainly made the city a better place. But in the 1980s and 1990s businesses and offices increasingly followed the lead of the factories and opted for a location outside the cities. The main reasons for this were the difficulty of access by car, the limited opportunities for expansion, and the lower price of land elsewhere. Although it is not applied equally strictly everywhere, the Nuisance Act also played a part in this process. Shops which required large floor spaces for their wares, such as furniture and DIY stores, shared the same motivation. Little new activity on a larger scale replaced them in the city.

Finally, the conventional city has been metamorphosed from the centre of society to an attractive tourist destination. In addition, a whole series of new means of communication have made physical encounters less and less necessary in day-to-day interaction. It is no longer necessary to go to the city to meet people when you can communicate with friends and colleagues by mobile phone, e-mail or internet. All the same, the fact that several city centres are still busy shows that people still like to meet one another in the flesh. Still, the city is no longer by definition the place for that – you can meet anywhere.

Genetic manipulation

It is not only the preservation of historic monuments that is freezing the dynamism of the city today; it is also happening because the city – or rather, the urban experience – is being rebuilt in a genetically manipulated form in the suburbs with the introduction of suburban genes. In terms of density, those districts are supposed to look like the city, to emphasise their urban quality. At the same time, however, a maximum of homes have to be built that take up land. The combination of these principles results in districts that are in fact nothing. They are not genuine cities, not only because the density and level of services are too low for that, but also because everything is designed too tidily; they lack the risky, the unexpected that is so much a part of city life. But they are not the suburbia that we know from Hollywood films either, because the density is too high for that and the homes are too fragile. So Vinex housing estates are like a genetically manipulated mouse with a human ear.

The increasing mobility is fragmenting cities and turning them into a network-like structure, bringing in its wake the redundance of a single centre. The big city is no longer the place where the action is set, and the centre of attention keeps shifting all the time. A recent Pepsi commercial is very revealing. An enormous dance festival is going on until sunrise in the middle of a desert. After a swig of Pepsi, the revellers all collect their belongings and run to a spot where it is still dark so that they can continue partying. It is the people, not the location, that count.

Of course, the city loses a considerable income through this exodus of people and activities. A lot of money is still generated by tourism: genuine tourists, day-trippers and the residents of the Vinex housing estates and outlying districts who still flock to the cities bent on consumption. The old façades in the **historic centre** are cherished and frozen in time to encourage the flow of cash that tourism brings in. As consumers of the city, these tourists are not aware of what is real or not. What does it matter anyway? A confrontation with a pastiche is still an authentic experience for the consumer. As Guy Debord summed up the nature of the **Society of the Spectacle** : 'Everything that was once lived directly has now become nothing more than a representation' (Debord, 1967). The result is a freezing of the evolution of urban building.

Evolution and transformation are natural processes that form an unmistakable part of urban developments and of culture in general. Until late in the nineteenth century cities were run without serious conscientious objections. Those parts which were no longer popular were demolished without regard for their historical value. Cities underwent a process of permanent renewal. Different architectural styles rubbed shoulders, or were sometimes stacked on top of one another in the cathedrals. Their age could be read off like the rings of a tree trunk. This process of permanent transformation is like a natural process of evolution. Within such a process, selection means adapting to changing circumstances. If the circumstances had remained unchanged from the first, evolution would have come to a halt at an early stage, before the arrival of homo sapiens.

Like nature, cities are constantly exposed to a changing context, and they have to adjust to this all the time, whether deliberately or through unforeseen mutations. This process has made the city strong and attractive. If the city is regarded as a living organism, then we can apply the dictum of the French philosopher Jean Baudrillard, (Baudrillard, 2000) to it: 'In evolutionary terms, victory belongs to those who are mortal and different'. All of our technology and science is aimed at countering decay and death. As an extension of this, we want to conserve the past that we are familiar with. It is precisely this idealising of the past that erases memory and destroys historical development. This endless reproduction of an arbitrary segment of time disavows the finitude of history and the directionality of time. The loss of the specificity of a moment and thus of a situation leads to indifference. After all, every experience can be relived, just like a computer game, so why should you care about specific moments, or about, say, the **dynamism of a city**?

Many cities in the West are dominated by the desire to stop the advance of time, so the historic centres are regarded as finished. Any possible mutation is ruled out as far as possible. Change and tension are not what tourists expect to find. The neutralisation of unforeseen developments consists of physically and, in particular, legally separating and labelling functions. While the historical cities were highly differentiated and derived a large part of their attraction from that very fact, today's districts are primarily monofunctional. The centre is for shopping, the business estates are for working, the residential areas are above all for sleeping. As a result, the districts are only used for a part of the day, there is no cross-fertilisation between the functions and chance events and/or encounters between the different users are more or less ruled out. Besides this functional separation, the cities also display an evident cultural and social segregation. There is no room for the unexpected.

It is gradually dawning on everyone that the separation of classes and functions is not ideal. Social mixing and the multifunctional use of space are therefore important premises of the new developments. However, this proves to be extremely difficult to bring about, especially in the new districts. Almost all of the Vinex estates have become the exclusive residential preserve of the ordinary middle classes and the programme of almost all the buildings has been defined so unambiguously that changes of function are virtually impossible. Vinex homes can never be anything but Vinex homes, most commercial buildings will always function as offices, et cetera. The dynamism of the city is consequently reduced to zero, and unless it is given an injection of new life, the city's days are numbered. The Franco-Hungarian architect Yona Friedman described the dangers of a city that fails to keep changing in his 1956 manifesto **L' Architecture Mobile**. Otherwise, Friedman argued, its users will turn their backs on it. More recently, theoreticians such as Michael Sorkin (in *Variations on a theme Park*; 1992) and Rem Koolhaas (in *Generic City*; 1995) have also relinquished the idea of the classic bounded city and proposed new definitions of the city: the **generic city**, the flexible city, the **network city**, and so on.

Generic city

'The city no longer exists. We can leave the theatre now.' These are the concluding words of Rem Koolhaas' essay *Generic City* (1995). According to Koolhaas, urban identity is a thing of the past. All cities look like one another – in particular because population growth has made the past 'too small to live in'. The classic city has been replaced by the generic city. 'It [the generic city] is easy. It does not require any maintenance. If it becomes too small, it simply expands. When it grows old, it just destroys itself and starts again. It is equally exciting – or dull – everywhere.' But it is not layered, since a streamlined city has no need of that. According to Koolhaas, the most important novelty of the generic city is that it does not renew itself, but simply abandons whatever does not work. While Michael Sorkin's *Variations on a Theme Park* (1992) still has a role for old city districts – though it is the unenviable one of being a habitat for the poor – according to Koolhaas they are practically written off. Until recently cities derived their identity from the old districts; the erosion of their historical significance makes cities bereft of identity and thus of history. The city has only two architectural typologies: the skyscraper in which the employed and wealthy congregate, and the slum where the poor live and fill up the ample space between the skyscrapers.

Vinex housing estate

How many generations of Vinex estates will have to be built before administrators realise that a culture exists by virtue of an undivided public space that is open to all, and that this public space only functions if people live there as well? Such a constellation of activities is called a city, and that is not the same as the separate development of a Vinex estate, a monitored shopping centre, business centre or recreation area.

For all three of them, flexibility – the ability to adjust and mutate - is what counts because the demands of the user are changing at an accelerating rate.

Of course, the question is then: How can today's functionally and socially splintered city be made flexible enough to restore a mixture of functions and income groups and to react to the changing context? If the city is to survive, a drastic transfusion is needed. It is not too late. The city is not dead yet, it still has enormous potential. Homes in or near the centre are very popular and thus very expensive. The proximity of cultural facilities, shops, catering, public transport and above all status turn out to be the strongest arguments in favour of living in the city. In addition, the city has its own kind of economy that thrives on personal contacts, on the one hand, and the emergence of breeding-grounds for new activities, on the other. The Dutch-American sociologist Saskia Sassen rightly claims that, in spite of all the new means of communication, the need for physical encounters has not disappeared. This is supported by the fact that many flexible offices have not been successful, and by the increasingly strong position of financial centres such as Tokyo, São Paulo and London, even though there is hardly anything more virtual than capital.

Today's cities seem barely, if at all, able to satisfy the demand for luxury apartments near the centre, the demand for flexible buildings, and the need for a healthy social, cultural and functional mixture and for breeding-grounds for new (political) initiatives. Demolishing and rebuilding the city is not a very realistic option, while leaving it to its own devices and allowing redundant parts die off – as is happening today in the American Edge Cities – is an undesirable option.

We believe that the addition of a new layer can breathe new life into the contemporary city. The roof would be an excellent basis for this. The flexibility that is so crucial to a city's dynamism is almost inevitable on this second level. Rooftop construction calls for the innovation of current building practices and points them towards an Industrial Flexible Dismountable (**IFD**) building method. In this way, existing buildings are not reduced to discarded plinths, but receive a new lease of life.

Various functions besides housing can be located on the roof. The roof is 'ordinary' – albeit ambitious – land for building, just as suitable for offices as for homes. The conference rooms by Coop Himmelb(l)au in Vienna (**office extension Falkestrasse**), by Erick van Egeraat in Budapest, and by Renzo Piano in Turin (**Lingotto**) are inspiring examples. These designs also show what an impact rooftop buildings can have on the building and even on the street below. A new wave of excitement enters the district: you see, know and feel that something unusual is happening at roof level. This form of rooftop construction is not parasitical – though one can imagine forms of parasitical buildings but symbiotic: the new building does not just extend the life of the old building on which it rests, but enhances its significance too.

In the Dutch urban investment estimate for 1999-2010, the fact that the city functions as a breeding-ground for new concepts and products is regarded as one of its main means of survival, but it requires special places; until recently former industrial sites, docklands and warehouses were ideal. But 'standard' housing has been built on almost all of these sites by now, or they have become so institutionalised that they have been neutered. The roof can fill this gap. Of course, it must not be built up with expensive studios, but with simple buildings or containers that may not even comply with all the **building regulations**. These buildings could become genuine counterparts of the (illegal) rooftop villages of Asia.

The rooftop buildings by French architect Jean Nouvel are more prestigious. First in Lyons and more recently in his design for **Les Halles** in Paris, he shows the rich potential of rooftop construction. In Les Halles Nouvel places a gigantic park including a swimming pool on top of the 26-metre-tall roof. This is not a new idea, by the way. Le Corbusier's Unité de L'Habitation apartment complex in Marseilles included a roof terrace with paddling pool. The design by Archipelontwerpers for the Black Madonna apartment building in The Hague includes not only penthouses but also a park and even an athletics track.

What all these examples show is that rooftop construction is dependent on function and place. Everything is possible somewhere. Thus it is possible to determine very precisely what the demand is for every location in the city. The next stage is to ask which new elements are capable of bringing the location in question to life: luxury penthouses, ambitious offices, new shops, or perhaps even greenery. It is not even necessary to build on top of every roof in order to make an impact at street level. Isolated interventions here and there – confetti urban development – are enough at first.

Building regulations

Rooftop buildings must comply with the regulations that apply to new buildings. Exemptions can only be granted if the politicians really want it.

The roof thus becomes an important vehicle of urban renewal. The street is reanimated because the new functions on the roof will create a

Fire safety rules

The building regulations are not mild, and that goes for rooftop buildings too, which are classified as new buildings. That means, for instance, that the fire-resistance requirement is 90 or 120 minutes, depending on the fire load and the height at which the building is constructed. This is surprising, because the structural fire safety of the rooftop building is largely dependent on the building beneath it. If the lower building collapses as a result of fire, no matter how fire-resistant the rooftop building is, it will collapse all the same. If it can be shown that the fire-resistance of the lower building is much lower than present-day requirements, the local authority can be asked to reduce the level of fire-resistance to that of the existing building.

Safety with regard to the spreading of fire is independent of the building below. The rooftop building simply has to comply with the safety conditions that apply to new buildings. The party floor and walls must therefore have a fire-resistance of 60 minutes. The regulations on the number of escape routes also have to be complied with. Although this is difficult (i.e. expensive), in fact it is very logical. No matter how exciting rooftop construction may be, it must not be allowed to become dangerous.

demand that could well be met below at street level. The presence of the prosperous occupants of penthouses or offices will be an enormous stimulus to local businesses. The simultaneous experience of different functions will be able to rejuvenate life in the city. The architectures of the rooftop buildings and of those beneath them will reinforce one another, just as the old and new functions and users will affect one another. In short, the result is an urban climate with typically urban, stacked constellations.

Stacking strategies

Stacking – the placing of functions vertically instead of horizontally – is a typically urban phenomenon. It is a clear-cut form of the more intensive use of space. The scale and complexity with which it is done is an index of urbanisation. Stacking can also be applied later to an existing city. In this way, the space in the city is used more intelligently and new functions can be incorporated into it. We can distinguish three stacking strategies.

The first strategy was introduced in 1925 by the Russian architect El Lissitzky. After high-rise building had produced all kinds of science-fiction type images of the city in the United States at the end of the nineteenth century, El Lissitzky designed a new type of high-rise building for Moscow: the horizontal skyscraper. This '**Wolkenbügel**' (literally Cloud Iron) consisted of three columns that were attached to one another by bridging volumes high above ground level. Lissitzky proposed building eight of these apartment blocks around the centre of Moscow to mark the entrances to the inner city.

If these apartment blocks were to be linked with one another, the resulting three-dimensional skeleton could be seen as a first step towards Yona Friedman's rooftop city. In Friedman's sketches for **La Ville Spatiale**, the columns have expanded to become immense three-dimensional infrastructures placed above the existing city. To give the city the dynamism that Friedman thinks it needs, fully dismountable floors, walls and housing units are then inserted into this spatial constructional frame, which becomes one of the permanent elements of the city.

Amsterdam, city on piles, a proposal by the artist John Körmeling, plays with a similar idea. He places a new city on piles, above the historic city centre that has been taken over by tourists, to provide space for accommodation, work and recreation for the people of Amsterdam. The two flows of people, who do not really want anything to do with one another, can thereby exist independently of one another.

The ideas of Yona Friedman and El Lissitzky reappear on a much more modest and realistic scale in a plan by MVRDV for **houses on piles in Ypenburg** that recall the raised **longhouses** of the tropics, and Archipelontwerpers' survival plan for the Black Madonna in The Hague.

The second stacking strategy is a little more complex. It involves raising an existing building to build something new beneath it. MVRDV came up with this strategy in their 3D-Groningen plan for **Pino Restaurant**. The Groningen local authority had asked them to look for building locations in the city as an alternative to a new, 2,000-home Vinex housing estate. One of the ways MVRDV thought of creating space in the city was to dismantle existing (often monumental) buildings and then to put them back again, but stacked and enhanced with new functions. The space created in this way in the city could be used for housing.

MVRDV made the same proposal for a monument in Austria that is on the UNESCO World Heritage List. After dismantling, a platform construction is put in place and the monument is rebuilt on top of it. A conference centre is built underneath this construction to cover the costs of the renovation and maintenance of the monument. The reverse process – placing a new building on top of the monument – would have been structurally impossible as well as seriously impairing the monument. Now it remains intact and is merely raised.

The third strategy is to add to an existing building. In many cases such additions are just extensions, like the **Art Gallery Giovanni e Marella Agnelli** by the Italian architect Renzo Piano in Turin, or **The Box** by his US colleague Eric Owen Moss in Los Angeles. Sometimes, however, they are unrelated elements, such as the **Parasite** by Rien Korteknie and Mechtild Stuhlmacher in Rotterdam, or the **penthouse** by **Richard Rogers** in London. There are situations in which incidents of this kind can turn into a raised ground level; in those cases, a city emerges at rooftop level. A well-known example is the Cambodian capital, Phnom Penh, where a village has been built on the roof of a square of apartment blocks. This slum, inhabited by people who lost everything in the war, accommodates bars, restaurants, small businesses and homes. It is an example of the growth of a stacked urban area on top of a traditional layer of buildings.

It is not likely that the roof will be used in this way in the West. MVRDV use the metaphor of a village in one of their roof designs, but this only refers to the extension of a home in which the parents' and children's bedrooms are separate elements (**Didden House**).

All the same, there are plans to provide thematic links between autonomous rooftop projects. In this case, small architectural interventions combine to produce an urban crescendo. It is not the familiar way of creating links in urban design, because it does not begin on a large scale and zoom in on the details, but sets out from a single object. Other projects follow later, step by step and independently of one another, and a play (including **rules of play**) of thematic references can be set up. Through their affinity in detail, vocabulary or programme, these relatively small projects will have an enormous impact on their surroundings; they generate a new vitality. Gradually, building by building, a new urban cohesion develops, without leading to increase of scale or a rigid intervention. This principle of thematic linking has many precedents, from Brunelleschi's work in fifteenth-century Florence to Bernard Tschumi's plan for the Parc de la Villette in Paris (1986). The most immediate references are the three façades that Palladio designed for three churches overlooking the Canale della Giudecca in Venice at the end of the sixteenth century.

This **stepping-stone strategy** has been applied on a small scale by Archipelontwerpers in **Scheveningen**.

Building services

The roof is far less immaculate than many would probably suppose. Quite a lot of shafts, such as the flue and ventilation pipes, discharge at rooftop level. Of course, you cannot just place a new building over them like that. They often have to be diverted and encased to emit their gases elsewhere. But they can also be channelled through the rooftop building. This calls for precision work, but is not necessarily more expensive. After all, the existing pipes retain their 'natural' course – they are merely extended – and it is easier to attach the pipes from the new building to the existing network. It is naturally important to calculate beforehand whether these pipes have sufficient capacity to transport the extra gases.

The rooftop building has to be connected to the drainage system too, and to be supplied with water, gas and electricity.

By giving new functions to a number of warehouses that were going to be demolished and placing steel penthouses above them that refer to one another, they gave the harbour a second life. The project began with a single incident, the construction of the steel **Harbour View** penthouse on top of two adjacent warehouses.

In Rotterdam, a strategy of confetti urban development has been proposed under the name of **penthousing**. The difference from stepping-stone development is that the rooftop buildings have nothing in common except that they are situated on the roof. Wherever possible in the centre, Rotterdam will support initiatives varying from rooftop extensions and penthouses to entire rooftop neighbourhoods, all in a variety of price categories, configurations and expressions. There is no theme, just a target of about one hundred homes. The project is intended to offer a solution to the monotony of the housing available and to provide a diversity that can match that of the canal houses in Amsterdam.

The premise in Rotterdam is thus completely different from that in cities like **Vienna** and **Berlin**, where the use of rooftops is also being promoted, but where it is above all a question of creating more surface area. What Rotterdam has in mind with this kind of urban development is clearly a case of rooftop buildings and not just of rooftop extensions.

Topping up versus rooftop construction

The only thing that topping up and rooftop construction have in common is their base, the roof. When it comes to purpose and ambition, they are very different. Topping up means building a new layer of homes on top of an existing building. This is how postwar tenement houses and flats are topped up. Homes of that period are usually fairly small, but their construction is sound. Making use of the roof was logical in itself, especially because it was combined with large-scale renovations which often altered the layout of the homes to bring them more into line with the requirements. The renovation had to be paid for from the income generated by the extra homes and the increased rents. The Trespa boxes that started to be placed on top of single-family houses in the 1970s to serve as two extra bedrooms belong to the same category of topping up. Although these extensions lacked any architectural ambition, they embrace some attractive architectural examples. A lot of attention has been paid to the architecture of the new layers, especially during the last few years.

So in principle there does not seem to be anything wrong with topping up. The buildings have been renovated, the original homes have been enlarged, and the number of homes has been increased. The space is thus used more intensively. The problem with topping up lies elsewhere. The topped up homes are often situated in neighbourhoods built in the 1950s and 1960s, which have been subject to economic and social erosion in the last decades. Average income earners have moved to a home with a garden in one of the outlying suburbs or Vinex housing estates. Their place has usually been taken by new residents with a lower level of education who have difficulty in finding jobs in today's service economy. The smaller purchasing power of these new residents and of those residents who have not moved, as well as the competition from the big supermarkets, have driven most local tradespeople out of business.

So what those neighbourhoods needed and need is in fact a different kind of intervention than the topping up of buildings. Topping up does not entail any enhancing of the programme. The rooftop homes are often aimed at the same target group as the original buildings. Besides, the location – the roof – is not used to the full. The layout of the rooftop homes is the same as that of the standard homes that have become common all over the country.

These are the main differences from rooftop construction. Rooftop construction adds a new social, functional and/or economic dimension to a district. Moreover, rooftop construction is never a standard assignment. It is always about formulating a specific (technical) answer to a (site) specific demand. The same is true of the specific spatio-functional programme for rooftop construction. Seen in this light, it would have been more interesting to build something on the roofs of the flats to be renovated that was lacking below that level.

If rooftop buildings are to compete with equally expensive **street-level homes** and attract people with higher incomes who want to live in the city but are not satisfied with what is currently being offered, standard layouts will not do. On the one hand, the spaciousness of the rooftop building must compensate the lack of a large garden. The home must provide an appropriately ample sense of space. After all, the way we live is determined not just by square metres, but also by our personal histories and emotions. The current shortage of space is as much perceived as real. On the other hand, advantage must be taken of the unusual location. Part of the pleasure of rooftop living is the view. The Harbour View penthouse by Archipelontwerpers in Scheveningen, for example, has a double routing in which both the inside and the outside staircase are important. The spacious terraces on different levels with a view of the Scheveningen harbour afford ample compensation for the lack of a garden. The extension of the office of Richard Rogers in London makes use of a complete glass façade fronting an impressive empty space for its view over the Thames. The glass terrace prevents the rather protruding building from robbing the parts below of too much daylight.

A different sector of the housing spectrum, a low-profile no-man's land that has been taken over by its users, can also add a new dimension to the district. Of course, a rooftop plan of this kind must

Street-level homes I

Developers believe that a two-storey house with a small garden is the ideal of everyone in the Netherlands. But if they all go and live in a house like that, the open countryside will be swallowed up. The low housing density means that facilities such as good bus connections, a station, a good shopping centre, a cinema, sports clubs and so on are not profitable. The occupants of the ideal homes on the ground still depend on the city, with all the problems of mobility that that entails, for work and recreation.

Street-level homes II

This has given birth to its counterpart: the rooftop house, and to this book.

comprise simple, parasitical housing, not expensive and ingenious architecture. For instance, more building can be done in the form of **tents**, sometimes supplemented with discarded and recycled building products. At their best, buildings like these resemble the minimalist roof extension of a building in London for the **Design Research Unit**. That design (1969-1971), for which prefab aluminium panels were mounted on a steel frame, was the brainchild of the architect Jan Kaplicky, who was working for Richard Rogers at the time. Deployed in this way, inhabited and situated away from the dull and the average, rooftop construction can be regarded as a spatial equivalent to **pataphysics**, the science of imaginary solutions. Situated somewhere in between the physical and the mental world pataphysical space is about the exceptions and accidents that no longer fit into the ordinary urban space but are essential for a city. It was precisely in the undesigned residual pieces of the city, the forgotten areas on the margins of the (historic) city, where the residential setting came to life and various interest groups did not end up in the politically correct middle-of-the-road compromise. Now that the outskirts of the city are being increasingly domesticated by the Vinex estates, the roof is the only escape route still available. This rooftop landscape of 'urban folds' offers sufficient space for all kinds of breeding-grounds and niches in the city. The mixture of different cultures can produce an effective impact.

To encourage this development, local authorities and other government bodies will have to interpret their regulations in a less rigid fashion. Entangled in a mass of regulations as it is, Dutch building practice virtually rules out the possibility of a sort of semi-legal rooftop village. To give free rein to experiments with new types of housing, the regulations on unambiguously rooftop penthouses should be taken a step forwards by being loosened up. They are new spaces with new demands, but above all with new aspects of experience that need designing anew. Of course, this is true of all experimental housing, including street-level versions. The tight budgets, the building methods they impose, and the compulsory regulations are obstacles to innovation in housing.

For both types of rooftop development, it is at any rate important for the building ground – the roof – to be as inexpensive as possible. Rooftop construction is expensive, and making the roof capable of supporting a building accounts for a substantial percentage of the **costs**. On the other hand, no land has to be purchased, and the urban infrastructure (except for **parking facilities**) is already in place. By shouldering some or part of that burden, local authorities may be able to deter prospective occupiers from making the most obvious choice of a penthouse or workplace location in the city. The second major difference from topping up is that rooftop constructions can cover a wide variety of functions. Depending on the demands of the particular location, offices, **parks** or **sports facilities** can be built on the roof. Rooftop construction must mark a location out as something special, and it does not make much difference whether it is so for architectural, social or economic reasons. Particularly in problem neighbourhoods, rooftop buildings can make a major contribution to rejuvenating a street. A more differentiated housing supply will also lead to a more differentiated composition of the neighbourhood community. There is bound to be interaction between new and old residents. Moreover, to put it bluntly, new money is pumped into these districts, which can be used to help to promote new economic developments. New functions are attracted, most of which can be accommodated at rooftop level. Of course, rooftop construction is not a panacea, but it can certainly make an important contribution to recovery.

Besides the economic and social benefits, there will also be an architectural interference between the old and the new buildings. Rooftop extensions literally sit on top of the building below and make use of the full depth of the plinth. Rooftop buildings will require a much freer use of the space on the roof. The depth of the roof will be used to accentuate the difference between old and new, and to create enough outdoor space. They are self-consciously autonomous entities that are placed on top of the building below. In *Housing: new alternatives, new systems* (1998), Manuel Gausa underlines the importance of such a structure: 'The strategy of combination and interrelation between autonomous organisms ("layers" of varied information) would allude to the urban form itself and its disintegration, as a harmonious and

Pataphysics

Pataphysics is a notion that was introduced by the proto-Dada French writer Alfred Jarry (1873-1907). Jarry (1911) defined pataphysics as follows: Pataphysics is the science of imaginary solutions, which symbolically attributes the properties of objects, described by their virtuality, to their lineaments. 'Pataphysics will above all be the science of the exceptional, even though people say there is no science except that of the general. It will study the laws of the exceptional and explain the universe supplementary to this one; or, less ambitiously, will describe a universe which can be – and perhaps should be – envisaged in place of the traditional one .... Current science is based on the principle of induction: most people have time after time seen one phenomenon precede or follow another and conclude that this will always be the case. But in the first place this only holds for the majority of cases, it depends on one's point of view, and is converted into a rule for convenience's sake.' Pataphysics is thus a 'science' that concerns itself with the chance occurrences and exceptions that are not covered by conventional science. If we replace the word 'science' by 'urban planning', the intention of rooftop construction becomes clear: it concerns itself with chance occurrences and exceptions that are not covered by conventional urban planning.

Jarry described his pataphysics as an epiphenomenon, as something that is extra, and that is focused on what generally escapes our notice. That includes the residual spaces, the hidden treasures, of the city, which could be found decades ago in the periphery of the city which lay beyond the reach of the planners. Now that they have been annexed by regulated suburbs, shopping centres and office complexes, we shift our horizontal gaze through 90 degrees and look upwards instead. Roofscapes are one of the few illustrations of a pataphysical space.

Seen against this background, rooftop construction will have to be totally different from what the monotonous and monofunctional topping up of the 1970s produced.

Pataphysics suggests a scientific basis, but it is in fact a literary statement. Here too there is an analogy with urban planning. A lot of information about the city is expressed in tables and diagrams, designed to give contemporary discourse the suggestion of being scientific. But a city is not the sum total of numbers and tables. In the last resort, it is about what people want to do with it.

coherent entity, into a new simultaneous landscape open to the union of disparate "messages"' and '... systems which are, in any event, particularly versatile precisely because of their mixed character, aimed clearly at making the systematic compatible with the seemingly aleatory'.

Rooftop buildings can assume any shape, but they will always be clearly distinguished from the plinth. The Harbour View penthouse and Rogers' office completely fill the area of the roof, which makes them conspicuously present. Many other rooftop buildings, on the other hand, are hardly visible from the street, if at all. But that does not make their presence less important. In fact, perhaps the reverse is true. You know that the roof is in use or suspect that it is inhabited. The rooftop building is visible from a certain spot, and that feeds curiosity. Rather than being fully exposed, the architecture is merely a felt presence that arouses curiosity.

The extra floor containing the whale-shaped conference room of the ING head office in Budapest is only visible from the street from one corner. The same applies to the Coop Himmelb(l)au conference room in Vienna – just a corner of it juts out over the edge of the roof. The implicit presence of these rooftop buildings makes an impact far beyond these sites and even these streets. In this way rooftop buildings grow to become an intensive experience of architecture, and the rooftop city (at least in the West) can expand to become the ultimate place for accommodation and recreation in the city.

From a distance the rooftop buildings are most likely to be visible. And so the skyline, which is currently dominated by horizontal lines, will be enlivened by rooftop buildings. The spontaneous **emergence** that we have in mind also means that it will have a less static character. This is related to the building technology, but above all to the basic aim of rooftop construction.

Generally speaking, topping up makes use of the same building methods as rooftop construction and the limiting conditions are the same. The building has to be light and capable of being constructed quickly, so timber frame or steel frame construction are obvious choices. In the case of topping up, however, there is hardly any room for the homes to be enlarged, because the roofs have to be filled with apartments in a single operation to maximise profits. Our ideal for rooftop construction does have such a possibility. That is why these buildings must be allowed to profit to the full from the flexibility afforded by specific building systems.

Building methods

No matter what advantages rooftop buildings may have, the constructional aspect of such projects is always tricky. The roof was not intended to be built on, and is not really suitable for it either. The room for manoeuvre in terms of constructional technique and architecture is both literally and metaphorically uncontrollable.

The first obstacle is formed by the construction of the original building. The roof construction in particular is not usually designed to take the weight of an extra home. In most projects the rooftop building is attached as directly as possible to the walls of the building below it. **Thames Wharf**, the rooftop office building by Lifschutz Davidson and Richard Rogers, demonstrates this principle in all its purity.

Besides the weight factor, stability (rotation) is also of great import-ance. To ensure a constructionally sound connection between the rooftop building and the existing one, a steel frame is often placed on top of the roof as a foundation. This frame has the advantage of evenly distributing the forces of the new building and transferring them to those parts of the building below that are the most suitable in structural terms. This frame creates a greater degree of freedom in the design of the rooftop addition. After all, the main supporting structure of the rooftop building no longer has to stand exactly above the supporting structure of the building below it. Moreover, this steel frame can be used to create good soundproofing because the rooftop building is not directly in contact with the building below. Finally, the space between the frame and the original roof can be used to house the new and existing pipes and cables. A disadvan-tage is that this intermediate structure raises the height of the rooftop building.

A frame of this kind was required for Harbour View because the two warehouses beneath it had to be linked together. Tensile bars con-nected the frame to the foundation to prevent the penthouse from 'blowing away'. A lift and an extra staircase were included in this and other rooftop projects in order to provide a new access route and sec-ond escape route. These constructional elements were also used to incorporate the features required to guarantee stability.

Instead of using a constructional frame, it is also possible to build immediately on top of the roof insulation and a compression layer, provided, of course, that the roof is strong enough to allow this. These two new layers form the basis of the rooftop building. These constructional solutions make it possible to place rooftop buildings independently of the structure beneath, as in MVRDV's Didden House to position them in relation to the existing structure beneath, or even to make them float above the existing building, like Renzo Piano's Art Gallery in Turin.

Whatever construction method is chosen, lightweight structural systems will be required in all cases. Although party walls and floors in the Netherlands are constructed to comply with the acoustic regu-lations (contact sound), so that most homes are actually more strongly constructed than is structural-ly necessary, the extra load on the foundation and party walls of the original building still has to be kept to a minimum. In most cases reinforcement of the party walls and the foundations – which is extremely expensive, of course – will therefore not be necessary. In the case of the **Meesteren Warehouse** in Rotterdam, however, designed by Japanese architect Fumi Hoshino, a completely autonomous construc-tion resting on a newly placed foundation had to be introduced into the existing warehouse building.

Emergence

Emergence is the phenomenon whereby relatively simple actions lead to one that is complex and even intelligent. It explains shared behaviour much more in terms of the individual.

An incidental rooftop building in a tidy street of uniform houses can change the look of the street considerably. Some will welcome this, others will be irritated by the intrusion. In a country like the Netherlands, where planning has been implemented on an appreciable scale, this often leads to serious emo-tional conflicts between supporters and opponents. In other regions, and in particular on other continents, nobody is bothered by such self-organising principles. But when the incident – the exception – becomes the rule, a new order emerges spontaneously above and in the street, neighbourhood or city. That is really the idea behind the rooftop city.

The monoculture of housing at the moment is enriched with a diversity of forms of building and housing. This first diversity in turn generates a new round of changes, leading to an increased complexity and variety in the surroundings. So this variety emerges as a sort of self-organisation from the interaction between various players. It is characterised by a measure of unpredictability. This type of order is spontaneous, and thereby unpredictable, rather than exactly formulated and imposed.

While the use of a lightweight structural system has its advantages, there are also aspects relating to building physics, such as soundproofing and heat accumulation, that call for extra attention. The latter can be a problem, especially in sunny parts, as the building may overheat unless measures are taken. In such cases the principles of the tropical roof are often applied: a second roof, with good ventilation beneath it, that shades the strong roof. In the penthouse by Archipelontwerpers in the **Witte de Withstraat** in Rotterdam, this second roof is fitted with solar panels to kill two birds with one stone.

Building process I

The conventional building process in the Netherlands consists mainly of filling tunnel formwork with concrete at an extremely fast pace. It is an economic process that enables housing to be produced relatively cheaply. The tempo indicates an industrial process, but the building activities themselves are pretty archaic. In fact, the characteristics of the process are fairly old-fashioned as well. While in intelligent industrial production the emphasis today is much more on serially produced one-offs, with the customer's demands influencing the industrially manufactured end product, serial production in the construction industry is mainly of identical objects. Variation is costly and is opposed or discouraged.

Other factors play a role in the choice of the constructional method as well. A rooftop construction site is not easily accessible. In addition, the duration of building work has to be kept to a minimum for two reasons. Nuisance in the street and to the users (if any) of the original building has to be limited as far as possible, and, since it is a relatively dangerous building site, the shorter the duration of construction work and the simpler the operations, the better for work safety.

The three limiting conditions (weight, accessibility, duration of construction work) effectively rule out traditional Dutch building methods – stacking and poured concrete (a building method in which concrete is poured on the spot). Both systems are too labour-intensive and result in heavy buildings. Opting for an industrial building method is thus logical, but it entails a certain paradox.

The desire of modern architects to industrialise the production of housing resulted in an enormous restriction of design freedom – and thus also of the domestic environment. The starting point – industrialised construction – made it necessary to define every component and to place it exactly within a hierarchy of assembly. Within this framework, it was logical to define the functional use of the home as precisely as possible. Especially in the West, the term 'functional' refers to the functional benefit for its users. This required a definition of how people function or live. And this is where the pinch comes. The absence of these definitions, the so-called objective term 'functionality' crumples and the desire to define a home is shown to be irrelevant (Vreedenburgh, 1992). After all, a home is not a home unless it is occupied, and the way it is occupied defines how it functions. This occupation of the home is a process that depends on period and culture, and is related to the personal preferences of the occupant. The urge to categorise in terms of function and efficiency for the industrial production of homes results in an enormous impoverishment and levelling of the pleasure of a home. The disadvantages of a building process industrialised along these lines are clear to see in the Netherlands. Although most of the homes in the Netherlands are not actually produced in a factory (though most of the components are), the building process itself is so streamlined and so rapid, and the final result is so fixed, that homes produced in this way display the characteristics of an industrial product of the nineteenth century – in other words, a great deal of the same, with no room for manoeuvre at all for the final user. Nowadays, however, computer-controlled industrial processes make it possible to make customised serial products. The kitchen industry is a good example of this. There are standard elements and components in all kinds of finishes and with all kinds of different accessories available from which to put your own kitchen together. If you are not satisfied with the result you can even have customised solutions made. Moreover, you can still perfect the kitchen you have ordered with all kinds of products that can be bought from a specialist or DIY stores.

An industrial approach is good for the turnover of the DIY stores, and vice versa: the growth of DIY activities increases the demand for readymade industrial products. It is in this paradox that the opportunities for an industrial approach to rooftop buildings lie.

If rooftop construction is to escape from the straitjacket of mediocrity – and that is one of the criteria of this building procedure – it will have to target serially produced customised products. This takes advantage of the benefits of prefabrication without imposing limits on the freedom of either the architect or the user. In our view, the architect's design can be put together on the basis of serially manufactured products with just-in-time delivery and on-the-spot assembly. It is not the products that need to be unique; it is their assembly to create a rooftop building that is unusual, just as a chef can make something special from ordinary ingredients.

The building tempo is high in this prefab approach, though the preparatory period is longer since the elements are now made in the factory. On the other hand, these building methods lengthen the durability of the building, which becomes literally more durable. This is because each component of a building has its own lifespan. They therefore do not all wear out at the same time. Since replacement is simple, maintenance and adjustments to the building over the course of time can be carried out with relative ease. In different interpretations of Industrial Flexible Dismountable building (IFD), the D stands for not only dismountable but also refers to **durability**. Although the dismounting and subsequent separation of the building materials in a recyclable production process is an important part of an industrial approach, little attention is paid to it here as yet. In our culture it is not common for something to be demolished or moved after a short time, but within the developmental process of the industrially manufactured home, dismountable building is a natural development. In fact, it ought to be possible to adjust any room in a building to a different use or to satisfy any other demand. Most built designs, however, lack this flexibility.

The present-day industrial building methods that are suitable for rooftop construction – **Dickholz**, timber frame on and steel frame construction – only allow a limited degree of freedom. They generally consist of flat elements that can be bent in one direction if necessary, although (limited) overhangs are possible and can be combined to form three-dimensional components in the factory. The more complex the form, the more interventions are necessary. So it is better to apply skeleton constructions for more complex forms. As the conference rooms by Coop Himmelb(l)au and Erick van Egeraat show, they can be made of steel or (laminated) wood. Steel makes it possible to design larger spans, of course, but freedom is not unlimited in this system either. The plates with which the skeleton is filled in are usually flat, and it is possible to bend the plates in two directions. Incidental experiments are being conducted at the moment to shape metal into double curved volumes by means of an underwater explosion. So before the demand for complex fluid forms or blobs can be met, we shall have to wait for a new generation of composite building materials that are lightweight, good insulators, as strong as steel, capable of being shaped into curves and that comply with the **fire safety rules**. These materials are already in use in the aeronautical industry. All kinds of developments are taking place in the field of new textile building materials too. A fabric made of carbon and metal textiles is shaped and then hardened with resins.

One way to reduce building activity on the roof to a minimum is to fully prefabricate the building. These have to be extremely light and small buildings, since not only must they put as little pressure as possible on the building below, but they also have to be transported. On the one hand there is the advantage of the lightweight character and very fast building process of rooftop construction; on the other there is the fact that it takes place to the detriment of the flexibility of the building. John Körmeling's Pioniershuisje [**Pioneer's House**], Luc Deleu's **sea containers**, containers which can be used as student housing, or Werner Aisslinger's **loft cubes** are examples of fully prefab rooftop buildings, although the first two are art objects and the latter is more of a design object. Aisslinger's website shows how he envisages the placing of his cubes. They are dropped on the roof by helicopter, but that is an oversimplistic approach, and he fails to indicate how a utilitarian link between the rooftop building and the structure beneath it is achieved and how the residents access their cube.
Like the construction, these are important questions. In many cases a new or extended lift has to be installed, and extra emergency exit routes have to be incorporated into the plan. As far as the **building services** are concerned, it is often possible to use the ones in the existing complex, provided the plumbing has sufficient capacity. This will not usually create a problem for the odd villa, but if several homes and/or offices are built on a roof, new piping will be required.

This all makes rooftop construction complex and thus expensive. It is therefore not surprising that a study carried out in Amsterdam – *Een extra laag [An extra layer]* – on the pros and cons of topping up came up with negative results. According to this report, demolition and rebuilding are preferable to renovation and topping up in many cases.
All the same, the First Penthouse company, which was founded in Sweden in 1992, has shown that fully prefab customised units are economically viable. This company manufactures complete homes in ten days and ships them to their destination. After being hoisted onto the roof by crane, the units are windproofed and waterproofed, after which the plumbing can be connected and the finishing can begin. Production is organised in such a way that the units can be adapted to the architecture of the building underneath. For example, the penthouse placed on a location in **Albert Court** in the centre of London is indistinguishable from the historic building underneath.

But of course, it is equally possible to have units that are completely different from the building below. They are expensive, but also have many advantages. The unit price in London, Paris and New York is between four and five million dollars. These are high prices by comparison with the cost of building the Harbour View penthouse in Scheveningen. In 1996 the price of building a surface area of 274 square metres was about 230,000 euros. And they are in demand. They cater for one of the ambitions of rooftop construction by introducing a new (architectural, economic and social) layer into the centre of the city using an efficient and innovative building method.

Amphionism

Books about cities usually consist of panoramas of the skyline or carefully selected views of a building or ensemble. Future urban developments are presented and discussed in the same way. The architect always presents his design in its entirety. But from the perspective of the passer-by, you seldom see complete panoramas or complete buildings. When you walk through the city, you always see fragments, arbitrary sections of parts of buildings that stand in front of and beside one another. The first thing that strikes you is that these fragments emerge from undesigned stackings. This composition – the arbitrary stacking – is thus only seen from the perspective of the viewer. If you walk through any city with this in mind, you will realise that a city consists of stacked structures: in this sense, the perspective of viewers in Rotterdam is not very different from that of viewers in Rome or anywhere else.

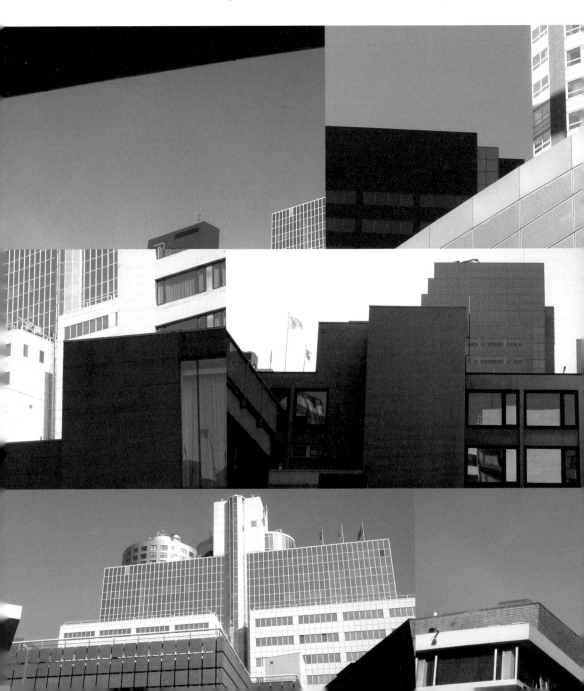

The poet Guillaume Apollinaire speculated on this, which he regarded as a new art form, in 1910. He called it amphionism, '... in memory of the strange power which Amphion possessed over stone and the different materials of which cities are made. ... The instrument of this art, and its subject matter, is a town of which one explores a part in such a manner as to excite in the soul of the amphion, or neophyte, sentiments that inspire in them a sense of the sublime and the beautiful, in the same way as music, poetry and so on. In order to preserve for posterity the pieces composed by the amphion, and so that they can be repeated more easily, he marks them down on a map of the city indicating the exact roads to follow.'

Rotterdam,

2004

Berlin

Fifteen years after the fall of the Berlin Wall, the city is still the biggest building site in Europe. During this period the attempts by urban developers to repair the broken city have been characterised by rigidity and an extremely selective historical consciousness. Under the motto of 'critical reconstruction', James Holbrecht's nineteenth-century blocks have been unimaginatively raised to the level of norm for the city. This critical reconstruction consists of a number of simple but rigid regulations concerning building lines, building heights, plot sizes, and sometimes specific prescriptions of materials. These regulations are applied with particular strictness to the blocks around the Friedrichstrasse and Unter den Linden. The blocks may not exceed a height of 22 metres, excluding two recessed roof storeys; the maximal total height is 30 metres. In addition, the window cavities may not occupy more than 49 per cent of the façade surface, and should be arranged in a grid. There is a further specific addition to the critical reconstruction in this part of the city: the façades have to be constructed of light-coloured brick. The worst disaster of this strategy so far is the Hotel Adlon. This old hotel dating from 1907 was the legendary and luxurious meeting place for artists, politicians, industrialists and aristocrats in Berlin. During the Second World War this building – like many others in the centre – was irreparably damaged and subsequently demolished.

In 1997 the architects Rainer-Michael Patzschke and Jürgen Klotz enlarged the old design to twice its former size, placed two storeys on top, and roughly copied the façade. This building is situated in Pariser Platz, a location that has come to symbolise the union of East and West after the fall of the wall. This set the tone for what is a paradoxical situation when seen in the light of this book. Everywhere in the centre you can see historic and quasi-historic new buildings with the two recessed rooftop storeys. These rooftop storeys determine the image of the centre, and the material used sometimes contrasts sharply with the material of the building beneath. In addition, many buildings in the city are being topped up. And, as in Vienna, every effort is being made to deny the existence of these rooftop extensions.

In spite of the attempt to combine functions in the city, most of the buildings in Berlin have a single function. Two projects with a high symbolic value (each within its own context) form yet another exception in the paradox that is Berlin: the Reichstag building and the Deutsches Architektur Zentrum.

The original Neo-Baroque Reichstag building dating from 1884-1894 by Paul Wallot already had a dome, but the interpretation that Norman Foster gave to the function of his dome during the transformation of this

building between 1994 and 1999 has meant that it too can be read as an
autonomous addition. This transparent dome is open to the public and
accommodates a restaurant and viewing terrace. What is more, light and air
enter the building through it. It combines many of the features that are a model
for rooftop construction, such as the stacking of functions and the use
of lightweight, prefab constructions.
The Deutsches Architektur Zentrum is less spectacular in architectural terms.
The centre is in a factory that has been entirely renovated by the architect
Claus Anderhalten. The former Stock plant is situated away from the centre in
the eastern part of the city. Besides the renovation, two new office wings and a
rooftop construction have been added. The steel rooftop construction contains
two offices and eighteen apartments.

Claus Anderhalten and Assman,

Salomon und Scheidt,

Deutsches Architektur

Zentrum,

Berlin

Erastus Salisbury Field,

Historical Monument to the

American Republic,

1867-1888

Museum of Fine Arts,

Springfield, MA,

The Morgan Wesson

Memorial Collection

OMA/Rem Koolhaas,

Hyperbuilding,

Bangkok,

study 1996

Hyperbuilding

According to Rem Koolhaas, a hyperbuilding is a city in the form of a building for more than 100,000 residents. This self-supporting structure is not primarily intended for implantation in existing urban conditions, but for locations that undergo a drastic expansion within a brief period of time. Koolhaas considers that Bangkok is the ideal context in which to try out the hyperbuilding. This design is the next step in the evolution from Wolkenbügel via Plan Opus, La Ville Spatiale to New Babylon and the Metabolists. The process embodies a shift in scale from (relatively) small to extra large to hyper large. With the exception of the Wolkenbügel and La Ville Spatiale, these buildings were designed for a new urban expansion, not for an intervention in the existing city. Rooftop construction, on the other hand, should in principle be carried out in existing urban conditions and therefore refers more to the character of emergence: stepping-stone or confetti urban development rather than hyperbuildings.

Harvey Wiley Corbett,

La Ville Future,

Stitch, 1913

New Babylon

In the 1950s, independently of Yona Friedman, Constant developed his first ideas about what he was later to call New Babylon. For many years Constant worked on a utopian proposal for a new form of housing and society as an alternative to functionalism – or, as Constant once called it in an interview with *Elseviers Weekblad* (Kelk, 1974), 'an antithesis to the lie society'. Constant's work consists not only of texts and paintings but also of maps (collages), models and design sketches. The latter are often set in an abstract situation: autonomous, linked structures above an open landscape. There are no sketches of his design proposals in an urban context. It is only in his maps that he makes statements about the development of New Babylon in the city.

What is striking is that his structures are placed relatively autonomously in relation to the landscape or a specific city. Constant's interventions in the map of Amsterdam are not essentially different from his proposals for The Hague, Cologne or Barcelona, for example. The cities function as an arbitrary, abstract background. In combination with his models, as a design they bear comparison with Friedman's informal visions.

Although they came from different backgrounds, Constant and Friedman share a number of conclusions that have lost none of their urgency forty years later. They are both fascinated by technological innovations to make people's lives easier. They both distrust prevailing views on urban development that are dominated by a naked functionalism. They see the city as a dynamic process characterised by freedom and playfulness.

Constant,

View of New

Babylonian sectors,

ca. 1971,

collection

Gemeentemuseum,

The Hague

They both welcome a flexible architecture that can be adapted to suit the wishes of the user. Constant summed it up succinctly: 'The future lies in mutability'.

The specific aspect of Constant – and at the same time the major difference between him and Friedman – was his social commitment. Constant drew up his plans within a revolutionary development and rejected the status quo. Constant and the Frenchman Guy Debord both played a major role in International Situationism for a number of years. Constant accused many architects of skilfully designing all sorts of cities of the future without abandoning the existing pattern of society. He thought that technology should be used above all to free people from work. That would also free them from their fixation on one and the same place to live and enable them to lead a more nomadic life. For Constant public amenities were of greater importance than individual space, and he reduced the latter to a minimum in New Babylon. While for Friedman the public aspect was no more than an individual choice, it was a recipe for the future for Constant.

While Friedman argues that cities should be elastic, in Constant's formulation the public space in New Babylon will be infinitely elastic: '... not only can he move through the space freely without being "rooted" anywhere, but he also moves through a space that is constantly changing in shape and mood and which therefore becomes unrecognisable in time. The fluctuation and the related disorientation mean that contacts between individuals can be created just as easily as they can be broken, resulting in an optimal scope of social relations.' Much of what Constant describes has developed in the course of time under different conditions. In today's society it does not have the positive connotation that Constant had in mind.

Constant,

New Babylon,

Amsterdam, 1963

collection

Gemeentemuseum

The Hague

Network city

The network city is the opposite of the compact city. The compact city concentrates all activities: home, work and recreation. The city functions as a magnet and if you do not live or spend time there, you do not count; at least, that is the feeling you get. That view is now outdated. You no longer live in the city, but just outside it. The city is dull (see Historic centre). And your recreation is no longer confined to a single city, but takes place in several cities.

Scientific American has investigated the relation between income and mobility, concluding that each dollar of a person's income is equivalent to an increase in mobility of one kilometre. Our prosperity gives us unprecedented mobility, which has liberated us from that single city and enabled us to be eclectic. It is not the city or the place that matters, but the people (the network) who are in that spot at that point in time, and thus in fact the infrastructure. Manuel Castells (1996, 2000) argues that the space of flows has secured predominance over the traditional space of place. The network city is a virtual city without limits.

Historic centre

What we call a historic centre refers to the classic city as we know
it from drawings, analyses and tradition – in short, from
theoretical constructions.
Of course, we can still visit the historic centre of a 'classic city', but the
most we experience in such a case is a contemporary slice of what was
once a city. In our mind's eye this classic city was multifunctional and
had layers of meaning. This is where things happened.
But the city – the historic centre – outlived its usefulness a long time
ago. It was too crowded and unsafe; there was no room for a home with
a garden, nor for a parking space. It was practically inaccessible by car
because of the continuous traffic jams. For all these reasons, the
original users left, and one by one the functions disappeared as well.
Only tourists still flocked to the city in search of a whiff of history,
authenticity, which became increasingly scarce and meagre because it
was faked. Still, tourists do not mind that very much. As consumers of
the city, they cannot distinguish between genuine and fake. And even
if they encounter a pastiche, the experience of that pastiche is still
an authentic experience for them.
But by now the tide seems to have changed. In other words, living in
the historic centre is coming back into fashion, particularly in
Amsterdam. Small apartments in the canal houses of the sixteenth and
seventeenth centuries, as well as in former working-class districts like
De Pijp and De Jordaan, are fetching huge prices today. The main
reasons for this are prestige and the desire to live close to where the
cultural life is. The fact that demand still outstrips supply may be an
opening for rooftop buildings, which are in more or less the same price
category as the expensive canal house apartments.

CIAM

In the CIAM (Congrès Internationaux d'Architecture Moderne) declaration of 1928, twenty-four architects called for a rationalisation of urban planning and architecture. Economic planning and industrialisation were to be made core concepts in the building of houses. The production of homes could be industrialised by aiming at simple forms. The meeting of 1933 was more important for urban planning. Led by Le Corbusier, it drew up a blueprint for the Modern City, which was later published as the Charter of Athens (CIAM, 1933). The functional city was characterised by a clear-cut zoning in which the zones were separated from one another by strips of greenery with, according to the Charter, 'high blocks at some distance from one another with flats, everywhere where there is a need to accommodate a large population density'.

That rigid functional division already came under fire in 1947, and this debate eventually led to the collapse of the CIAM. Architects like Alison and Peter Smithson, Aldo van Eyck and Jacob Bakema did not believe in the four functionalist categories (housing, work, recreation and transport) and sought a relation between the physical form and socio-psychological needs instead. '"Belonging" – identity – leads to the enriching experience of neighbourhood. The short and narrow alley in a slum succeeds, where ambitious urban redevelopments often fail.' These architects eventually joined together to form Team X.

El Lissitzky,

Wolkenbügel on

Nikitsky Square,

1924

> MVRDV,

Costa Iberica,

Aristotles's Law,

1998

TION = 7.500.000   AREA = 38 KM2   DENSITY = 250.000 INH./KM2

Yona Friedman,

La Ville Spatiale,

1958-1962

L' Architecture Mobile

In 1956 the Franco-Hungarian architect Yona Friedman launched his ideas on mobile architecture with sketches and a manifesto. Many of these design sketches show clusters of homes that float above the existing city in a three-dimensional structural frame. This frame – the infrastructure – is one of the fixed components of the city in Friedman's view. How this frame is filled in with floors, walls or housing units must be entirely flexible. In this way big cities can evolve and be intensified or extended as required.

Friedman's manifesto describes the dangers of a city that is not constantly changing. He claims that a city that bores people has no future: the residents (and users) will abandon it – which is what is actually going on today. Although Friedman's city certainly does not resemble Rem Koolhaas' generic city at all, in a certain sense they share a particular standpoint: it is the users who dictate how the city should look and function. The city adapts to the requirements of its

occupants. However, Friedman argues for dismountable buildings or for buildings that are so designed and constructed that they can accommodate a very wide range of different functions. Koolhaas, on the other hand, sees the users discard their city. So while Friedman regards the city as flexible but in a progressive sense – like a piece of elastic that has lost its elasticity – he also considers that the city must constantly adapt to the wishes of its users, but he has more confidence in the city as a bounded entity, as a finite body within which that flexibility has to be built. His first designs, Span Over Blocks (1957-1958) and La Ville Spatiale (1958-1962), which offer a preliminary outline of his ideas about placing buildings on top of an existing city, should be considered as technical proposals rather than actual designs for a particular situation. To underline his theory – that existing cities must be intensified in order to evolve – he made the design for Paris Spatial in 1959. This design consists of a number of sketchy montages of a city on top of the city of Paris. Projects in a similar vein are Constant's New Babylon, the artificial ground level in Frankfurt-Römerberg by the architects Georges Candilis, Alexis Josic and Shadrach Woods, and the principles of John Habraken's Stichting Architecten Research Foundation for Architectural Research, the SAR.

John M. Johansen,

The Mummers Theater

(Oklahoma Theater Center),

Oklahoma City,

1965-1970

< MVRDV,

Costa Iberica, Sand City,

1998

Black Madonna

The centre of The Hague has been like a building site for a number of years. In the 1980s Carel Weeber's master plan for the Wijnhavenkwartier was the basis for new policy. One component of this was the Black Madonna housing complex, which was completed in 1985. For a long time the building stood in isolation in the city. It was not until the 1990s, after Richard Meier had built his town hall and Rob Krier's Resident quarter had been built that the Black Madonna finally received the context for which it had been designed. In the course of time, however, views on architecture and urban design changed. The Black Madonna came in for particularly heavy criticism, and the sitting council called for its demolition.

These plans led to a lot of commotion and discussion, and various alternatives were proposed for the Wijnhavenkwartier, most of which set out to show that there was no need to demolish the Black Madonna. It is in this force field that Archipelontwerpers drew up a plan to preserve the Black Madonna and to breathe new life into the complex with rooftop housing.

The plan consists of a rooftop landscape of about 75 rooftop homes, a rooftop park with sport/fitness facilities, a children's playground, and a crèche. These homes are mounted in a steel paling that rests partly on the roof and partly on supports that must be placed in the courtyard. The building will be encircled by a moat, and the courtyard will be made accessible from several sides. Extra staircases and lifts will be constructed in this courtyard, and all other staircases will be extended.

The homes are to be built of lightweight, prefabricated steel frames and are flexible in design. A lot of space is left open between and beneath the homes so that the courtyard can receive sufficient and varied light. The whole plan envisages facilities for hanging gardens and solar panels between the homes. This open ground plan, the large amount of differentiation, and the light steel façade finish are in sharp contrast to the closed building with its black ceramic tiles. This difference between the black plinth and the airy rooftop level displays a difference in design, but above all an alternative view of housing.

Archipelontwerpers,

Project for Black Madonna,

The Hague,

2001

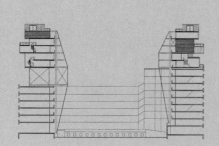

Les Halles

Rem Koolhaas, Winy Maas, David Mangin and Jean Nouvel were invited to make a new design for Les Halles in the centre of Paris.

To compensate for the lack of greenery and the enormous building volume required on this site, Maas and Nouvel propose a large raised park. Since there are already many floors with diverse functions beneath ground level, this represents a highly intensive and urban form of programmatic stacking.

Ateliers Jean Nouvel,

Design for Les Halles,

Paris, 2004

< Yann Arthus-Bertrand,

Cattle raising near Fukuyama,

Japan

Kurt Handlbauer,

Golf links, Arakawaku,

Tokyo, 2002

Sport facilities

Since it is just a raised ground level,
the rooftop can be used for anything,
including sport. Golf facilities have
been installed on a fairly large
number of roofs in Japan, England
and the United States. Sometimes they
are midget golf courses, sometimes
putting greens, and a few even afford
room to practice strokes. Of course,
there are high nets around the edge
of the roof.
Many a chic hotel has a swimming
pool on the roof; even more spectacular
is the canoe pond on the roof of
a block of flats in Osaka, Japan.
And there are buildings with rooftop
basketball fields; one even has a
hockey pitch on the roof.
The roof can be used for other kinds
of recreation too. In Tokyo a gigantic
roller coaster has been built on
– or rather over – the roof facing the
façade of a number of blocks of flats.
Some roofs in the US and Japan,
especially above shopping malls,
have fairground attractions and
playgrounds for children.

NL Architects,

The Basket Bar,

Utrecht, 2003

Horizontal differentiation I

Manuel Gausa's *Housing* (1998) is a plea for horizontal differentiation in buildings. He argues that this makes the buildings livelier: 'Systems which are in any event particularly versatile precisely because of the mixed character, aimed clearly at making the systematic compatible with the seemingly aleatory'. This horizontal layeredness is an automatic consequence of rooftop construction. But there are also new building projects that consist of different, seemingly autonomous layers, in which it is precisely the combination of the different forms that makes the buildings so attractive. The apartment complex in Sittard designed by Neutelings Riedijk Architecten is a good example of this. The building is clearly broken into three. The heavy plinth supports the intermediate section, with somewhat lighter materials and details, while sculptural, timber-clad penthouses are situated on the roof. The building thus combines the urban developmental, architectural and socio-economic advantages of rooftop construction.

Another recent and extremely successful example is the Basket bar by NL-architects on the campus of Utrecht University. A basketball field has been placed on the roof of a bookshop and café. The fact that the building beneath was a café that served meals was an obstacle, because a large kitchen requires good exhaust ventilation, and in this case that could not be taken straight through the roof. The problem was solved by using the poles of the cage around the basketball field as a chimney.

Neutelings Riedijk

Architecten,

Apartment complex

Prinsenhoek,

Sittard, 1995

Society of the spectacle

In his book *La société du spectacle* (1967; *The Society of the Spectacle*) (1967) the theoretician Guy Debord warns of a society based on images. 'When the real world is turned into images, images become reality …. Everything that is immediately experienced has been removed from the representation. The spectacle is in general, as the concrete reversal of life, the autonomous movement of the inorganic.'

Debord regarded his society of the spectacle as the extension of the alienation that is inherent in industrial society. In this society, people are degraded to the status of passive observers, who move through society like semi-manufactures on the conveyor belt of a process of production. In the 1960s, simultaneously with the Canadian philosopher Marshall MacLuhan, Debord stated that the world is becoming a global village in which images and their manipulation hold sway. Unlike MacLuhan, however, Debord saw the global village as nothing more than a village, with all the narrow-minded prejudices that go with it: narrow-minded control, conformism, boredom and isolation. So the spectacle is not a waste product of a world of observers, but deploys images to show the social relation between people. Debord distinguishes two variants: the concentrated spectacle of the dictatorship, and the diffuse spectacle of consumer society.

Kurt Handlbauer,

LAQUA Amusement Park,

Korakuen,

Tokyo, 2003

Variations on a Theme Park

Michael Sorkin's *Variations on a Theme Park* (1992) claims that the most important function of the historic city was that of a meeting place. Physical encounters in a specific place are becoming less and less necessary with all today's means of communication. You no longer go to the city centre to meet people, instead you communicate with friends, colleagues and relatives via your mobile phone, e-mail or internet. And if you want to see someone, you do not do so in the centre; you can meet wherever you like. The increased mobility enables you to travel to the point where the action is at that moment. Sorkin considers that the city will come to resemble television: the location-bound identity of the city is destroyed to make way for a continuous urban design field in which you can zap as you please. The new city is uniform; the same is true of buildings, which in theory can be placed in any city, and in any arbitrary spot in that city. 'Locality is recognised efficiently by the croque-monsieur on the McDonald's menu in Paris' (Sorkin, 1992). Besides its uniformity, the architecture in these cities is supposed to radiate above all a happy-face cosiness. Risk of any kind – which is inherent in the traditional city that has evolved instead of being carefully planned – has to be banished. Neither tourists nor businessmen want to be confronted by anything unforeseen. The city is a secure theme park.

Proposal for a cooperative
apartment building,
ca. 1920

< bbvh architecten,
Joris van Hoytema,
Design for housing project
The seven heavens.
Illustration P.J. Bleichrodt,
2001

John Körmeling,

Car-free City,

2002

Wild housing

Proposal for a skyscraper
as utopian device,
published in *Life*,
October 1909

The debate on wild or market-led housing, which was launched a few years ago by Carel Weeber, is an obvious reaction to the over-organisation of town and country planning in the Netherlands. Only in a culture where housing is so regulated can a debate on 'wild housing' emerge. This canalised form of freedom of choice has led and continues to lead to homes with practically identical ground plans, arranged to form tidy rows or attractive blocks, with a an architect-designed façade, and turned into a 'cool' Vinex estate through the interference of a committee of supervisors.

Steigereiland in Amsterdam was supposed to be a site for wild housing. Within a rigid urban development plan, in which even the boathouses were arranged in tidy rows, the owner occupiers were allowed to do what they liked on their own plots of land. But the imposition of a grid and supervision by a quality team prevented it from ever becoming wild or exciting.

Le Corbusier's Plan Obus – the kilometres-long project for buildings on the Algerian coast without any fixed interior design (*une système complètement des fonctions du plan de la maison*) – and SITE's High Rise of Homes plan – a car park with villas and gardens of the occupier's choice instead of cars – already offered more freedom for a genuinely individual design of the interior. In principle they did not impose any (architectural) quality criteria. These plans, however, are still marked by a tightly regulated structure – apparently that is necessary to achieve urban design coherence. Of course, this structure limits individual freedom enormously. The attempt to organise wild housing within a tightly regulated plan is already a contradiction in itself. When we survey the entire discussion of wild housing, we find that hardly any change has taken place in the building process. Talking about it worked as a sort of sublimation, and provides many developers and local authorities with a political alibi for not putting it into practice.

Smart Tower,

Capelle aan den IJssel,

2004

SITE Architects,
James Wine,
Water's Edge, 1981
collection
Laura Carpenter,
Dallas, Texas

> MVRDV,
Dutch Pavilion Expo 2000,
Hannover, 2000

John Körmeling,

Zaanstad cottage,

2004

Pino Restaurant

A new Vinex housing estate threatens to spring up on the northern edge of Groningen. Nobody is really happy about it, but there is no space inside the city limits for the two thousand homes that are needed. Nevertheless, MVRDV was commissioned to investigate whether these homes could be built in some way or another in the historic city instead. The firm of architects was successful, albeit it in a rather unorthodox way. MVRDV followed two strategies: linking existing building blocks by apartment blocks built above them; and dismantling buildings, often monuments, and then rebuilding them in a stacked form. The two thousand homes that are needed can then be built in the space that is released.

It looks above all like an attractive, theoretical study, but it is likely that one of the proposals is actually going to be implemented. The monumental building on Hereweg which houses the Italian restaurant Pino will probably be dismantled. MVRDV has designed a large apartment block for the original site. The old restaurant, fully re-stored, will be reconstructed on the roof of this new building.

MVRDV,

Design for Pino Restaurant,

Hereweg,

Groningen, 2004

Parasite I

During the cultural event Rotterdam 2001, there was a poisonous-looking green building on top of the lift shaft of the Las Palmas building in Rotterdam. It was designed by Rien Korteknie and Mechtild Stuhlmacher from LP2 and was constructed using Dickholz elements. The original idea was to use a steel skeleton, but that turned out to be far too expensive. Dickholz has constructional as well as financial advantages. The wall elements are delivered to the building site ready for use. It took three and a half days to assemble the Parasite. The panels are simply bolted together. The foundation was the conventional one of steel girders attached to the lift shaft. The lift shaft provided access to the new home, and the terrace was attached to the shaft. The finishing took another four weeks. The finishing on the outside is in Kerto, which is a pine plywood like Dickholz, but waterproof. Though small in size, the building contained two (very small) living rooms and a kitchen on the first floor. The way the kitchen surface and the dining table merge into one another is very well done.

Korteknie Stuhlmacher
Architecten,
Parasite,
Rotterdam, 2001

Parasite II

A parasite (from the Greek para, 'beside', and sitos, 'grain, food') is an organism that lives in or on another organism and draws its nutrients from it. So it lives off its host, though in most cases the host does not become seriously ill as a result. In fact, the reverse may be true for the species as a whole. The pressure of infection can bring about a larger genetic variability, which enhances the chances of survival of the species.

Symbiont

Symbiosis (from the Greek sun, 'together', and bios, 'life') is the constant, close physical association between two dissimilar organisms. Mutualism, in which both organisms (symbionts) benefit from the association, is its most positive form. Parasitism, in which the host organism is harmed (to some degree) by the guest organism, is its most negative form. Rooftop extensions are often described in the architectural literature as parasitic constructions, but given the added value of a rooftop home for such a host, symbiont would be a better description (Melet, 1997).

Dickholz

Dickholz or Lenotee is a structural timber consisting of layers of pine glued together to form a sort of plywood – though composed of planks instead of veneers – that can be as much as 25 cm thick. The thickness guarantees strength and rigidity, as well as accounting for a large percentage of heat resistance. The manufacturer claims that heat resistances of up to 2.5 m^2 k/w can be obtained. The thickness also provides the required level of fireproofing. In the event of a fire, the outer layer will be carbonised and thereby protect the rest of the wood. The system is already widely used in Germany, where it leads to fairly traditional German homes.

The Parasite in Rotterdam (2001) by Korteknie and Stuhlmacher was the first project in the Netherlands in which Dickholz was used for the frame. A major advantage of this system is that the components are prefabricated. In the factory they are sawn to a maximum of 5 x 25 m. The sawing is computer-controlled and customised, down to the rebates and the openings for doors and windows. All that has to be done on the rooftop is to fit the light elements together.

first floor

ground floor

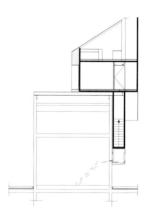

section

Parasite III

Parasite in the Parasite project stands for Prototypes for Advanced Ready-made Amphibious Small-scale Individual Temporary Ecological houses. The project originated in 1999 as an international initiative in Malmö, Sweden. Thirty European firms of architects are taking part by designing these kinds of temporary houses for forgotten spots on, in and between buildings.

Parasitism versus symbiosis

Architecture journals often refer to rooftop
buildings as parasites. This implies that they
are regarded as isolated architectural objects.
Such an interpretation, however, completely
ignores the influence that these little pinpricks
can have on their surroundings. In our view,
they should be regarded as examples
of symbiosis.

John Körmeling,

Pioneer's House,

Rotterdam, 1999

Studio Aisslinger,

Werner Aisslinger,

Mobile Loft cube,

Berlin, 2003

Loft cubes

The de luxe variant of the sea container, the loft cube, should conquer the flat roofs of the post-war buildings in the capitals, according to German designer Werner Aisslinger. His aim is not simply intensification: he sees his loft cubes as the ideal homes for the nomadic way we live today.

The fully prefab 6.6 x 6.6 metre objects are placed on the roof by helicopter. The frame is made of wooden honeycomb panels finished with white polystyrol.

Two variants have been developed: the house and the office. The price of the house is about 55,000 euros.

Nevertheless, a number of important questions remain unanswered. For example, what about access to these homes? The loft cubes can be placed on the roof by helicopter, but are the new occupants supposed to reach them by helicopter as well? How they are attached to the building below is also unclear, while one of the artist's impressions of the loft cubes even includes a swimming pool.

One gets the impression that the loft cubes are in fact no more than luxurious rooftop extensions. Although Aisslinger's principle is different, it does not look as though autonomous homes can be constructed with loft cubes.

Witte de Withstraat

Archipelontwerpers has designed two model projects in Rotterdam: on Witte de Withstraat, and Maasstraat. In terms of expression, each project is the opposite of the other, intended to provide references for the discussion about penthousing in Rotterdam. Based on the experience that the firm of architects acquired in designing several penthouses in Scheveningen, these IFD model projects explore the limits of the architectural and urban design aspects as well as those related to production technique. A roof-top landscape of five basic penthouses is planned for Maasstraat, and a very complex and expressive villa for Witte de Withstraat.

In terms of programme and composition, the five penthouses Maasstraat refer to the Scheveningen types. The homes are designed to cater particularly for the expectations of new city folk: large homes for small households. They have spacious, flexible ground plans with the possibility of an extra guest room or a home office. The large living room, including an open space, is divided over several levels. Large terraces are added, connected by an external stairway, enabling different routes through the house. Thanks to this approach, the penthouses can compete with homes and gardens at ground level outside the city.

Hierarchy

It is too often assumed in the design disciplines that you proceed from large to small, from rough to fine, and never vice versa. Within this hierarchy, a zoning plan is higher than an urban development plan, which is in turn higher than an architectural design. The architectural design is higher than an interior or detail, and so on. Reality, however, often shows us a different sequence.

Various scenarios have been devised for the penthouse on Witte de Withstraat, varying from one large penthouse and two smaller apartments to a continuous space to live, work and exhibit in. Both locations are in the city centre and are difficult to reach as building sites. To shorten the time required to build them, they are made of prefab building components ready for dry assembly.

The challenge of the two projects is to show how an industrial process of production can be used to produce a highly personal home environment. To make the logistics of this serial production of one-offs manageable, the architect for the Witte de Withstraat project cooperated with the IAAA to develop a special algorithm using the Artificial programme. A random series of configurations was generated, one of which was selected and elaborated further.

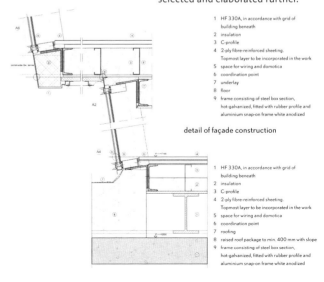

1 HF 330A, in accordance with grid of building beneath
2 insulation
3 C-profile
4 2-ply fibre-reinforced sheeting. Topmost layer to be incorporated in the work
5 space for wiring and domotica
6 coordination point
7 underlay
8 floor
9 frame consisting of steel box section, hot-galvanized, fitted with rubber profile and aluminium snap-on frame white anodized

detail of façade construction

1 HF 330A, in accordance with grid of building beneath
2 insulation
3 C-profile
4 2-ply fibre-reinforced sheeting. Topmost layer to be incorporated in the work
5 space for wiring and domotica
6 coordination point
7 roofing
8 raised roof package to min. 400 mm with slope
9 frame consisting of steel box section, hot-galvanized, fitted with rubber profile and aluminium snap-on frame white anodized

Archipel Ontwerpers in
collaboration with IAAA,

Artificial penthouse

Witte de Withstraat,

Rotterdam, 2000

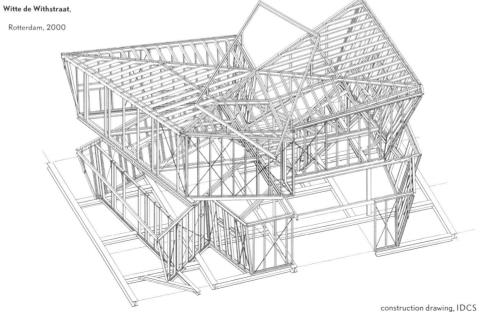

construction drawing, IDCS

Artificial

Anyone who wants to build in a more flexible and varied way has to participate in the building process and to give the impression of being personally responsible for every detail of the building that is to be designed. It is necessary to design at a higher level of abstraction and only specify rules of play and limiting conditions; the specific elaboration is left up to the final user or to chance.

There is a rich tradition of this more distanced approach in the arts. Ever since Marcel Duchamp, more and more artists have taken up the challenge to produce non-intentional art, which was already implicit in Immanuel Kant's view that our rationality is more limited than our cognition, i.e., that we know more than we can articulate. All kinds of very different tendencies have developed protocols for the creation of works of art by more or less autonomous processes. They are set in motion by the artists, but the final result is not known in advance: écriture automatique, action painting, biological processes, aleatory art. Sol LeWitt (1969): 'The artist's will is secondary to the process he initiates from the idea to completion .... The process is mechanical and should not be tampered with. It should run its course'.

The clearest example of a distanced approach is algorithmic art, a term for a work or category of art that can be described by a rule of calculation (an algorithm) that is laid down with mathematical precision – in other words, complex and unpredictable processes are defined by means of fully explicit rules, which are then consistently and accurately implemented by the computer. In theory a simple algorithm can be carried out by hand, but when we speak of algorithmic art we usually have in mind computer-generated art. By means of an algorithm you can define a large category of different images with perfect precision, for example by indicating that all possible variants within a certain pattern must be systematically gone through. The algorithm is a 'meta work of art': the mathematical characterisation of a collection of possible works of art (Scha and Vreedenburgh, 1994). A similar question is at issue in architecture as in art, with the difference that the production process (namely, the need to keep costs to a minimum) is even more constrictive in architecture than in art.

To avoid the production of monocultures, designers have to be able to link pluriformity with a precisely described process of production. Herein lies the potential of Artificial, a program written by Remko Scha and Jos de Bruin from IAAA (Institute of Artificial Art Amsterdam), which is capable of generating arbitrary works of art in this way. In a process of this kind, the designers draw up rules of play that determine which situations are possible. In this way the architect can take decisions on scale, rhythm or the repertoire of applicable elements for a specific context.

Each specific situation receives a morphology of it own. This is how the penthouse in the Witte de Withstraat in Rotterdam was designed. Archipelontwerpers formulated a number of rules of play, which IAAA then converted into algorithms. Afterwards arbitrary spatial configurations could be generated. One of them was the basis of the design that Archipelontwerpers went on to elaborate.

The use of computer programs in the design processes is no longer unusual. There are a good many architects who work with them, like Greg Lynn, Foreign Office, Ben van Berkel, Lars Spuybroek, and Kas Oosterhuis. Their method is called 'parametric design'. They introduce several parameters (from highly specific, such as the orbit of the sun, to highly abstract), which will subsequently affect the shape of the final building. This places the legitimation of the architectural object outside the sphere of influence of the architect.

But in most cases the architect will reassert his authority by eventually selecting and freezing a particular configuration from the process. The term 'fluid architecture' refers mainly to the blob-like designs in which this can result, and not to a permanent state of change.

The difference in the use of Artificial for the penthouse in the Witte de Withstraat lies not so much in the use of a different kind of software, but rather in the reason for using it. Archipel-ontwerpers were concerned in this project less with the complexity of the architectural object than with breaking open the (industrial) process of production in which architecture is imprisoned.

In their view, this process could be driven in a formally unambiguous way by means of algorithms, while the result would be an unpredictable industrial series of unique products. This approach may prove to be extremely suitable when it comes to giving rooftop construction a chance.

Steel frame construction

Steel frame construction is derived from timber frame construction. The wooden horizontal and vertical beams are replaced by cold-formed, zinc-coated C, L, omega, Z and U sections. They are finished with plasterboard and plywood, and the combination of the components provides the necessary rigidity and strength.

Steel frame construction is older than is often supposed. Steel frame was developed in 1949 by the Philips designer Alexandre Horowitz. The system has become relatively popular in Australia and Great Britain, but it has hardly been used in the Netherlands so far. That is now changing, partly thanks to the number of rooftop buildings that are under construction. Many of the advantages of timber frame construction are also to be found in steel frame construction: the material is light, the components are prefabricated, and the system is easy to assemble. Steel, however, can be used for larger spans than standard wooden beams. In addition, steel is impervious to water, enabling detailing with smaller tolerances. The problems connected with building physics and fire safety, however, are larger than in timber frame construction. A steel frame gives way within five to ten minutes, so the cladding has to provide the necessary protection.

Creative cities

Diversity and complexity, in other words, an abundance of
possibilities, are the inextricable symptoms of a well functioning
city. That is not surprising. Nature too shows us that more
complex systems have a greater chance of survival than
simple ones.

When new connections and specific orders arise from chaotic
flows and forms of information, we speak of innovation.
Innovations are thus by definition unpredictable, though it is
possible to create a climate that makes innovations more likely
to happen. This climate apparently often likes to nest in then
o-man's-land between order and chaos. This is where formal
planning and bureaucracy meet the informal and spontaneous
side of society. This climate is predominant in the old outskirts
of the city or in its disused warehouses and industrial complexes.
It was precisely these less tightly organised locations that often
proved to be breeding-grounds for small start-up businesses
and for alternative forms of housing. Traditionally these are
the areas where a large diversity of multifunctional hybrid
forms have emerged. Unfortunately, such areas are becoming
increasingly scarce. With the Disneyfication of the centre and
the Vinexisation of the outskirts, there is hardly anywhere to
escape to. This certainly does urban creativity no good.

This is yet another argument for turning our gaze ninety
degrees and going in search of new city limits: the rooftop
landscape. If these locations are not occupied by regulated,
tidily arranged layers of homes but by people who live in
symbiosis – or, in this context, perhaps 'as parasites' would be
more accurate – a more informal and creative picture can
emerge in the city.

Ortner & Ortner,

Haus Rucker.Co,

Balloon for Two,

Vienna,

1967-1992

> Starck Network,

Asahi Beer Hall,

Tokyo, 1989

ONL (Oosterhuis, Lénárd),

Parasites,

Rotterdam, 1994,

image: Ilona Lénárd

Tents I

The human race has a long tradition of nomadism. Our ancestors moved from one place to another in search of better hunting grounds, a better climate, better (new) partners, and better conditions. Although human settlements date from around 6000 BC, the urge to keep moving on is still in our genes. Fear and pragmatic considerations tie us down to one place, but the urge to be 'genuinely' and 'completely' free continues to dog us, and once we are given the opportunity to escape from our humdrum daily existence, we exchange our home for a tent, caravan or dormobile.

Some peoples have escaped the Neolithic revolution (agriculture). In the deserts of North Africa and the steppes of Mongolia, tribes like the Bedouin roam – partly under compulsion – from oasis to oasis, from market to market, just as they always have done. They take their belongings with them. Although their draught animals (camels or yaks) can carry enormous burdens, the items which are not for sale have to be kept as light as possible, because every pound of dead weight means a pound less of commodities. They thus have good reason to find the most efficient design for their homes. Following their intuition, they constructed tents of woven fabrics and ropes that only had to take up the tensile stress, while they used branches that they found on the spot for the heavy pressure [compressive] elements. This yielded a construction that was easy to erect, dismantle, fold up and transport.

The use of fabric makes the tent intrinsically a clever invention in terms of building physics as well as construction. The fabric is made of wool from goats, camels or yaks and offers exceptionally good resistance to the extreme climatological conditions in the desert. By day it can be thirty degrees cooler in the tents than in the scorching sun. Not only does the fabric of the tent prevent penetration by infrared radiation, but the hairs of the skins stand on end from the heat, thereby releasing the warmth from the tent. When it is cold at night, the hairs lie flat again and retain the warmth produced by human bodies and the campfire. Moreover, the woven skin radiates the heat that has been absorbed during the day into the tent, which thus remains relatively warm.

We have lost the art of such intuitive construction; nowadays we build in accordance with a maze of laws and regulations. This has not been to the benefit of the buildings. Most of them are static, cumbersome, and not very intelligently composed. Rooftop construction may require us to trust to our instinct again. Although the circumstances are completely different, the mechanical limiting conditions for rooftop construction are not so different from those for constructing this type of portable (mobile) building. Rooftop construction also calls for light materials that can be rapidly put together. What is more, rooftop buildings are preferably flexible and dismountable – supplementary criteria that are perfectly in line with the most suitable building methods under such circumstances.

Tents II

Adriaan Beukers from the air and space travel division of the Technical University Delft has been calling for airplanes and cars made of composite textiles for years. There are many advantages. They are extremely light and strong, and can in principle be moulded in any shape. The textile is the support: the new, light semi-manufacture is easily transported to the roof. Once the textile, which is coated on both sides with foil, has been arranged in the desired shape – on the one hand,

it is prefabricated in that different parts are sewn together in the factory, while on the other hand its final shape can be determined on the spot by adjusting the temporary frame – the air is extracted to create a vacuum.

Wind turbine blades are already made in this way. Once a coating of resin has hardened on the textile, the 'building' – the outer shell – is seamless, and thus both windproof and waterproof. The same procedure can be used for the inner shell. The space between the two shells can be used, just as it is today, for the required thermal and acoustic insulation and to accommodate extra functions, thereby making the tent smarter to use.

This will already have taken place at the stage of choosing an intelligent mixture of threads from which the textile is to be woven, for instance metal wires as well as composite fibres. This reinforces the tent and automatically creates a Faraday cage; it also enables all kinds of items such as electrical wiring and flexible water, gas and heating pipes to be incorporated into the skin. These services can then be tapped from any point in the tent. Sensors determine which parts of the tent are in use and thus require heating and light. The space between the inner and outer shell also has to be used to make the tent self-sufficient. A hydrogen cell, or a compact water purifier, for example, are techniques that have been tried and tested by now and that can easily be incorporated into a home of this kind. If rooftop buildings are made self-sufficient, they really do become symbionts. Until then they may be in architectural symbiosis, but are still parasites on the facilities of the building beneath.

It is even conceivable, as in the City Fruitful plan by Kas Oosterhuis and Ashok Bhalotra, to process the waste materials from the building beneath in the rooftop building to the benefit of the entire complex.

Michael Rakowitz,

Parasite Shelter,

Cambridge, 1998

Courtesy Michael Rakowitz

Extension Design Research Unit

In 1971 the London firm of architects Design Research Unit invited Richard Rogers to design a rooftop extension for its new premises. The so-called zip-up system proved to be ideal for this purpose: the low weight level meant that the new floor could be placed on top of the existing structure of the building. The aluminium panels are placed on a steel frame. The uninterrupted span creates an opportunity for a large, open, light working space. Jan Kaplicky's photomontage presents a witty version of the concept.

Richard Rogers Partnership,
Design for extension of
Design Research Unit,
London, 1969-1971

Jan Kaplicky, photomontage

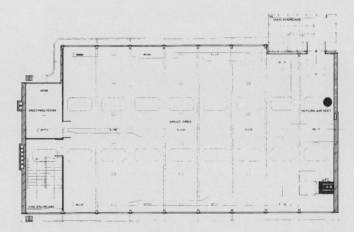

floor plan

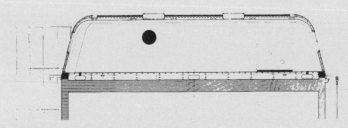

section

Stefan Eberstadt,

Rucksack House,

2004

> Air borne extension,

unknown architect

Timber frame construction

Timber frame construction owes its structural qualities to the monocoque principle, which combines relatively slender, timber structural elements (horizontal and vertical beams) with thin and non-rigid claddings such as waterproof plywood (outer wall) and plasterboard (inner wall). The combination of these elements results in rigid, boxlike components (floors, walls) that can be assembled to produce a rigid and strong construction. In principle the façade can be finished in any material, from brick to metal sheeting.

The system has a number of important advantages. A timber frame home is between 25 and 30 per cent lighter than a brick one. Moreover, it can be prefabricated almost in its entirety. The elements are transported by lorry, hoisted onto the roof, and assembled. Until recently this building method was only used for one-family homes, but after experiments in Scandinavia, multi-storey apartment blocks are now being built with a timber frame too. The acoustic and fire safety problems that seemed to be an inevitable consequence of the lightweight nature of the elements have been solved by means of flexible and detached constructions.

Annika and Hakan Olsson,

Penthouse Albert Court,

London,

2000

Santiago Cirugeda Parejo,

The mutant architecture,

home extension,

Seville, 2000

Santiago Cirugeda Parejo,

The mutant architecture,

capsule,

Seville, 2000

Chicago, 1986

Business parks

The Netherlands is faced with a shortage of building land for business parks. The existing ones can barely expand, and it is becoming increasingly difficult for businesses to move to a suitable location. The shortage is so acute in the province of South Holland that the local authorities have joined with the Chamber of Commerce to set up Decor (Dutch acronym for Durable Economic Use of Space) to supervise the restructuring process. All 450 existing business parks in this province are to be investigated. The existing supply, the level of services provided, and the organisation of the public space no longer satisfy the present-day requirements of the world of industry and commerce.

Decor is a platform where discussions take place on investments in joint services for such matters as security, waste collection, cleaning, park management and energy.

The search for space also has a high priority.
In our view, the 'new space' should be sought above all in stacking functions. This stacking can vary from relatively small rooftop additions to building a new layer on top of a business park in the form of a self-supporting construction. This new space should certainly not be used just for businesses, but should accommodate other functions too such as housing or recreation. This is a way of breaking with the monofunctionality and dullness of business parks. Although there are still obstacles to be overcome in the field of technology and investment, regulations (on noise pollution) form the greatest of them all. On the other hand, the environment will be the main loser if the current extensive development of business sites is allowed to continue unabated.

Andrezej Wejchert,

Smithfield Village,

prefab unit on chimney,

Dublin, 1996

Lingotto

The Fiat plant in Turin, Lingotto, was built in the 1920s and was regarded at the time as one of the foremost and most up-to-date industrial complexes. The process of car manufacture started in the basement and ended on the roof, where the cars were given a few test runs before going back to ground level to be sold. Of course, the test track on the roof was an early form of rooftop construction. Fiat decided to close the plant down in the 1970s, and the question was what to do with this enormous complex (almost 500 metres long, with a volume of one million cubic metres), which had dominated the centre of Turin for decades. Renzo Piano was commissioned to turn it into a multifunctional complex. Lingotto now houses an auditorium, an exhibition space, part of the university, a shopping centre, a hotel, and a cinema, as well as still serving as the head office of Fiat.

The premise was the preservation of the plant's monumentality. Piano unquestionably succeeded in this, although the glass bell-jar (la bolla) seems rather out of place. It is the counterweight to a helicopter landing pad and is intended as a conference room for the happy few who arrive by helicopter. The bell-jar has an exceptionally finely detailed glass façade with awnings on the inside. So it literally hangs above the industrial complex and looks down on it. Although that will certainly not have been Piano's intention, this bell-jar has thereby acquired a somewhat creepy air.

Renzo Piano Building Workshop,

Redevelopment Lingotto complex,

Turin, 1983-2003

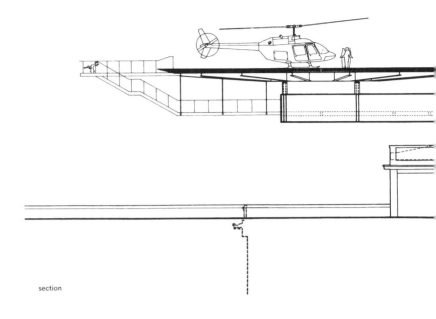

section

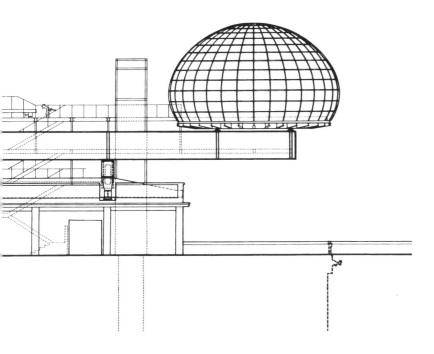

Art Gallery Giovanni e Marella Agnelli

The Agnelli family ís Fiat, so Giovanni Agnelli was almost morally obliged to devise new functions for the enormous Lingotto plant when it closed in the early 1980s after having dominated the city of Turin for decades. Renzo Piano was commissioned to turn it into a multifunctional centre. One of the latest additions to the complex is the gallery for the works of art that Giovanni and his wife Marella have collected over the years. The Pinacoteca is situated in the northern section of the former industrial complex and is accessible through the museum shop. Above the shop, three floors of the original complex have been reserved for temporary exhibitions. The so-called casket (lo scrigno) stands with four enormous steel feet on top of the reinforced concrete complex. The details and dimensions of the steel supports are clearly adapted to Lingotto's fascinating coarseness. The casket, a mere 450 square metres, has thereby been detached from the building below and would offer a view of the former plant, were it not that the museum does not have many windows, although this is sufficiently compensated by the hanging staircase and the panoramic lifts that give access to the casket.

Unlike the construction below it, the roof is extremely refined and detailed. As the Pinacoteca has been detached from the plant, so the roof seems to have been detached from the main volume, thereby accentuating the floating character of the museum even more. Piano calls this roof the 'floating glass carpet'. The roof combines beauty with functionality: it admits plenty of daylight, but the warmth of the sun is removed from the air and absorbed by four different layers. The topmost layer, which hangs far over the edge of the volume, consists of 1,700 white sheets of glass. Below them are horizontal glass elements, aluminium louvers, and a white translucent ceiling.

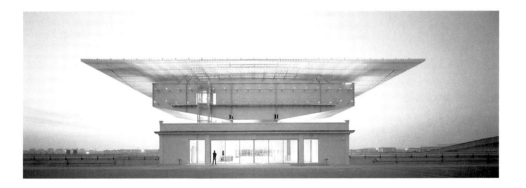

Renzo Piano Building Workshop,

The Giovanni and Marella Agnelli Art

Gallery, in the Lingotto complex,

Turin, 1983-2003

Thames Wharf

In 1983 the Thames Wharf location in Hammersmith, London, consisted of decaying, abandoned warehouses dating from the beginning of the last century. They were ripe for demolition. In the following year Richard Rogers was given the assignment of converting these warehouses into business and office spaces as well as designing a housing complex next to them. Besides an unusual apartment block and the converted warehouses, his intervention resulted in two gems: the penthouse of John Young, his business partner, and the semi-circular steel rooftop building, designed in collaboration with fellow-Englishman Lifschulz Davidson, into which Rogers has moved his practice.

The office is situated in and on top of an old warehouse. Rogers makes use of the whole warehouse, but the reception area is in the semi-circular rooftop building, where all Rogers' models can also be seen. But it is the view that catches the eye. The striking, light semi-circular construction has retractable cotton blinds to provide shade from the sun. The glass terrace is very clever, enabling the daylight to penetrate to the floors below.

Richard Rogers Partnership
and Lifschulz Davidson,

Office of Rogers Architects,

Thames Wharf,

London, 1987

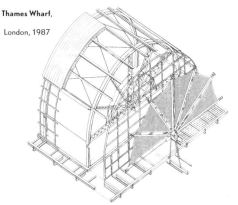

Opera House

In 1986 Jean Nouvel won the competition for the new Opera House in Lyons, France. Remarkably, unlike the other architects he retained the original building, or rather, three of the four original façades. Apart from the façades, however, practically everything else was demolished. An almost entirely new building has been built immediately behind the nineteenth-century colonnade. In this sense the Opera can be regarded as an example of a quasi-rooftop building. The materials and

use of detail bear all the hallmarks of Nouvel – a lot of black reflective glass and reflective natural stone. The architect's ingenuity lies in how he has merged the old with the new. The dark glass ensures that the areas behind the arches are experienced as black holes in the daytime, so that the historic appearance of the street has not been altered. In the evening, however, the activities shine through the enormous expanses of glass and the original building is much less prominent. This metamorphosis is a tremendously effective device.

All the same, in the daytime too the rooftop building leaves no doubts as to how drastically the building has been renovated. Nouvel placed an enormous curved steel roof on top of the building. Clad with steel profile plates and glass, it creates a razor-sharp and uncompromising contrast between old and new. The kitsch female statues that have been placed in front of the glass do nothing to temper the transition. Surprisingly enough, in spite of, or because of, the two evidently different parts of which it is composed, the building is experienced as a unity. The rehearsal rooms are located in the rooftop building. That is probably as surprising a choice as its form and material, since it is one of the most beautiful parts of the building with the best view. A restaurant would not have been out of place here. The view from a restaurant however, is primarily from the inside towards the outside, offering passers-by in the street a fairly passive picture. Rehearsal rooms, on the other hand, invite curiosity from the outside towards the inside, and will thus attract people to the performances.

Ateliers Jean Nouvel,

Opera House,

Lyons, 1993

Horizontal differentiation II

Jean Nouvel's Opera, but above all the home of the architect Manuel Herz in Cologne, are typical examples of what seem to be rooftop buildings. A new building has been erected behind the original façade that rises above the existing façade and merges with it in an intriguing fashion. Strictly speaking, these are not rooftop buildings, or course, but in terms of architecture and urban planning they have the same impact as a genuine rooftop building.

< Manuel Herz,

Legal / Illegal,

Manuel Herz House,

Cologne, 2003

Whitney Museum

The original Whitney Museum of American Art in New York was designed by Marcel Breuer in 1963 and is one of the highlights of his oeuvre. Besides this building, the museum includes a number of adjacent premises, the so-called brownstones. Although the latter also form a part of the protected cityscape, they proved to be less impregnable than the Breuer building. The programme put forward by the client in early 2001 hinted that OMA was expected to come up with such a brilliant design that the authorities would even agree to the demolition of the brownstones. However, they turned out to be ideal for exhibiting prewar art, and OMA incorporated them into the new design.

The expansion of the museum, resulting in a doubling of the total floor space, was to cover not only a number of exhibition spaces but also the areas that were to form a part of the Experience. These areas, among which OMA included the infrastructure, the restaurant, the café, the library and the bookshop, had to be conquered by the artists who wanted to show here. The name Experience refers to their ambivalent character: these areas were not in the first instance designed for exhibitions, but would eventually be used for that purpose.

Because OMA left the original buildings intact, there was only a small area left to build on. In order to come up with the requisite number of square metres, the OMA design would first rise upwards before dramatically overhanging the existing buildings. The extension is at a distance from the Breuer building and the brownstones, and is thus not a genuine rooftop building, but it is an impressive example of a horizontal differentiation implemented at a later date, an effect that can also be achieved with genuine rooftop buildings.

The three buildings retained their original characters in the OMA design, but by linking them to one another at various levels – for example, on the third floor, where the lobby was situated – they blended to form a unity.

Initially OMA thought of using concrete for the difficult construction of the enormous overhang. It also looked into the possibility of using steel, but both OMA and the structural engineer, Cecil Balmond of Arup, found concrete purer in architectural and constructional terms. Window openings have been applied at functionally appropriate points in the supporting concrete outer layer, as well as at points where the pattern of forces allowed them. That premise has given the façade a strikingly free composition.

Understandably, the conditions after 11 September 2001 changed so drastically that OMA was asked to provide a new design that was less exuberant and less manifest. But the momentum was gone, and in February 2002 the museum scrapped its plans for a new extension.

OMA/Rem Koolhaas,

Extension Whitney Museum,

New York,

design 2001

level 2

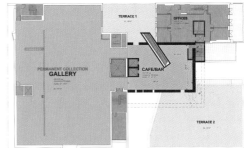

level 4

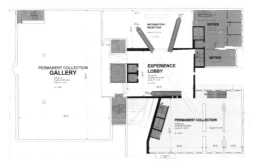

level 3

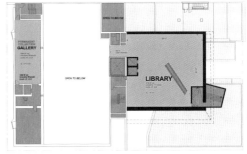

level 4.5

OMA/Rem Koolhaas,

Extension Whitney Museum,

New York,

design 2001

section exhibition area

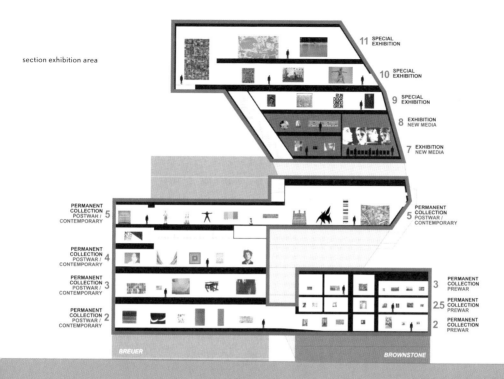

11 SPECIAL
EXHIBITION

10 SPECIAL
EXHIBITION

9 SPECIAL
EXHIBITION

8 EXHIBITION
NEW MEDIA

7 EXHIBITION
NEW MEDIA

PERMANENT
COLLECTION
POSTWAR /
CONTEMPORARY 5

5 PERMANENT
COLLECTION
POSTWAR /
CONTEMPORARY

PERMANENT
COLLECTION
POSTWAR /
CONTEMPORARY 4

PERMANENT
COLLECTION
POSTWAR /
CONTEMPORARY 3

3 PERMANENT
COLLECTION
PREWAR

2.5 PERMANENT
COLLECTION
PREWAR

PERMANENT
COLLECTION
POSTWAR /
CONTEMPORARY 2

2 PERMANENT
COLLECTION
PREWAR

BREUER

BROWNSTONE

section

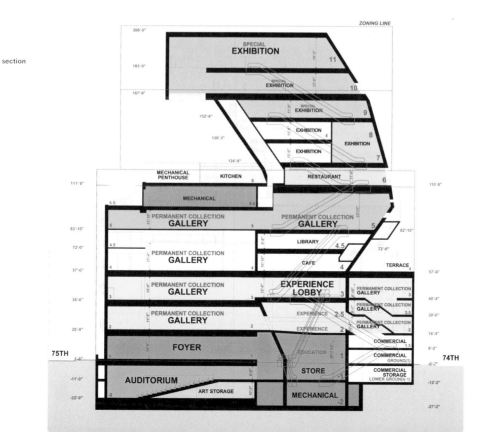

The Box

Eric Owen Moss Architects is housed in a simple wooden shed from which a strange volume, rises into the air. This rooftop structure consists of three parts. It actually begins on the ground floor with the cylindrical reception area which cuts open the roof of the shed, as it were, to create the opening for the structure on top. Behind the reception is the staircase that leads first to the roof terrace and then (via the open air) to The Box. The fact that you have to go outdoors before you can enter The Box is a typical and effective example of an architectural route.

By means of a construction made up of robust sections partly laid over the cylindrical glass roof above the reception area, The Box is kept separate from the lower building. The Box is less of a box than it name suggests. As one might expect from Moss, the spatial figure has been distorted. An unusual detail is the cut-out corner with a sheet of glass casually tacked on. As in the original building, the materials and details are coarse, making the penetration of the wooden shed look like an act of violence. It is not clear whether The Box has landed and partly sunk through the roof of the shed, or whether it has penetrated the roof from the ground.

The Box is a conference room. The large openings afford a view of Century City to the west and of the inner city of Los Angeles to the east. Of course, the unusual rooftop construction attracts a lot of attention – especially at night, when The Box is spectacularly illuminated from below. At the same time it is evidence of the strength of rooftop buildings: a completely normal shed is suddenly given an architectural charge.

Eric Owen Moss Architects,

The Box,

Los Angeles, 1990

ING Head office Budapest

One-and-a-half extra storeys were required to accommodate the programme for the head office of the ING bank in the nineteenth-century monumental building on Andrassy Ut in Budapest. The architectural advisory committee was against the idea. It wanted to preserve the original look of the street and keep the influence of Western culture to a minimum. The Dutch architect Erick van Egeraat was nevertheless granted permission for the extension, on condition that it would not be visible from the street. Van Egeraat therefore kept the original zinc roof and placed the completely glass roof of the extra floor diagonally on top of it. The glass roof has an unusual construction because Van Egeraat wanted a maximum of transparency. The supporting construction is therefore made of laminated glass that rests on the steel main construction via stainless steel supports. However beautiful it may be, it is not really an example of rooftop construction, but 'the whale' is. It lies on and hangs from the glass roof, as if it has fallen through it. The shape was even wilder in the preliminary sketches, when it looked even more like one of the bizarre and ominous objects by the US architect Lebbeus Woods. In the course of the design process, however, the forms grew more curved and gentle, and the object was nicknamed the whale because of its tactile zinc skin. The shape was created by sawing laminated wooden beams into the desired form. At rooftop level the space between the ribs is almost completely filled with glass. This is where the board of directors meets. It affords a panoramic view of Budapest, where most buildings are of more or less the same height. The space beneath the roof is almost entirely coated with roughly welted zinc cladding. This is a closed meeting place for the personnel.

Erick van Egeraat Associated

Architects,

ING Head office and

Nationale Nederlanden

head office,

Budapest, 1994

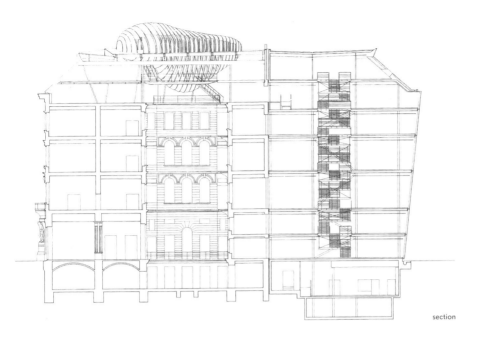

section

Office extension Falkestrasse

What is probably the best-known rooftop building is in the Falkestrasse in Vienna. The Schuppich Sporn & Winishofer firm of solicitors commissioned Coop Himmelb(l)au to extend the premises with a conference room, three offices, a reception area and a secretariat. The Viennese firm of architects drew their inspiration for this project from the street name. The building (1988) has all the aspects of a bird, but if it looks like a bird, it is a fragmented one: a bird that has been ripped apart and roughly put back together again. 'Roughly' certainly does not apply to the details, though, for they are wonderful. It applies more to the surfaces, which are practically all rectangular. The building is a concrete construction but consists mainly of steel and (both transparent and translucent) glass. Not only the shape but also the site are remarkable, as the building has been placed on top of a traditional Viennese building and is hardly visible from the street. Only the 'beak' made of tubular steel protrudes beyond the edge of the roof.

The building is both an architectural wonder and a clever technical construction. It had to be, because it introduces asymmetrical forces into a brick building. That is why a construction of steel and reinforced concrete was developed, which transfers the load in a controlled manner to the brick façade between the two chimneys. The most eye-catching structural element is the tensioned Gerber girder, which forms the backbone of the building. The smaller lattice girders determine the form of the rooms next to the conference room.

section

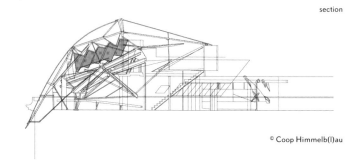

© Coop Himmelb(l)au

Coop Himmelb(l)au,

Office extension,

Falkestrasse,

Vienna, 1988

Vienna

Rooftop extensions has accounted for a large proportion of block redevelopment being carried out in Vienna. Building on the roof provides an opportunity to achieve a social mixture and a higher density. To date, however, it has mainly resulted in topping up operations in which the new layer is hardly distinguishable, if at all, from the layer below or from the buildings in the vicinity. A striking exception is Redtenbachergasse where an apartment building is being constructed next to and on top of an old factory. The sale of the land gives the factory the financial elbow-room to modernise. A large area of the roof will also be covered with plants. This kills two birds with one stone, since improvement of the public space is another important component of the cleaning up operation. All the same, these plans have hardly any architectural value. Rüdiger Lainer's penthouse and, of course, the conference room by Coop Himmelb(l)au, both in Vienna, are much better examples of the potential of rooftop construction.

Coop Himmelb(l)au,

Office extension,

Falkestrasse,

Vienna, 1988

Bias Architecten,

Extension Maritime Hotel,

Willemskade,

Rotterdam, 2000

construction drawing

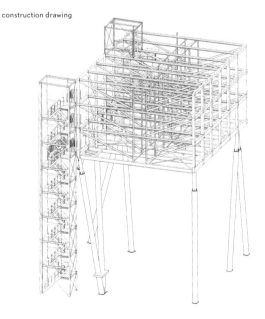

The Bridge

A large bridge construction appropriately named The Bridge floats above the new Unilever head office, at the entrance to the Feijenoord district in Rotterdam. The building of this striking design is part of the redevelopment of a strip of land beside the River Maas. The owner was granted permission to expand his office premises on condition that housing was built on the location at the same time. That is why the new offices have been placed on top of the old building. The office building consists entirely of modular components and has the status of a model IFD construction. The steel structure of the building, which is about 32 metres wide and 132 metres long, consists of sixteen elements that were partly transported to the site by water. After they had been fitted together on the building site, the whole object, including the concrete floor sections, was was raised by hydraulic lift trucks and put in place 25 metres above the floor of the old factory complex, and then finished. The whole construction rests on steel supports. The façade components were attached from inside because there was no room for scaffolding. The factory's 24-hour production process continued uninterrupted throughout the building period. The office, designed by JHK Architects, comprises four storeys and is extremely transparent. A central entrance hall with lifts and a staircase links the old factory with the new offices.

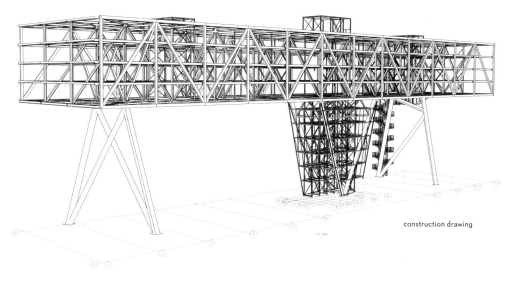

construction drawing

JHK Architecten,

The Bridge,

Rotterdam,

implementation

commenced in 2002

JHK Architecten,

The Bridge,

Rotterdam,

implementation

commenced in 2002

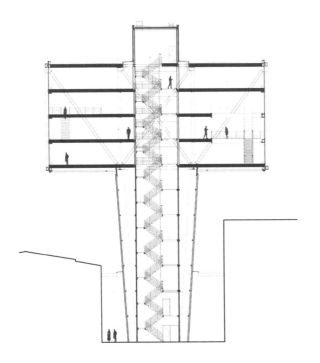

Archipelontwerpers,

Design for Mali Tower,

The Hague, 2000

Sea containers

Sea containers, which are now in use as student accommodation, are very suitable for placing on the rooftop. The Belgian architect-artist Luc Deleu's Orbino project (1988-2002) shows what beautiful shapes can be created with them. Of course, these homes are not very practical, and besides, they are small and hardly comfortable. Still, as temporary homes – as parasites which conquer the rooftop landscape and introduce a new layer of functions into a district – they can function very well. Moreover, they can be delivered ready for use, thereby limiting rooftop activities to a minimum. They can be removed just as easily. This layer of rooftop buildings can thus adapt very rapidly and efficiently to demand, and will therefore be in continuous movement.

Luc Deleu,

Orbino,

1988-2002

El Lissitzky,

Der Wolkenbügel,

1925

collection Van Abbemuseum,

Eindhoven

Wolkenbügel

Strongly influenced by the Suprematist paintings of Malevich, the Russian architect, typographer and exhibition designer E. Lissitzky ended his career as a painter with the creation of prouns: projects to establish the new. These drawings and paintings comprised cubes, squares, lines and curves derived from geometry and modern architecture, which were placed autonomously as if they floated on the plane surface in an infinite space. These prouns were just an intermediary between painting and architecture, and had a great influence on Lissitzky's proposals for the Wolkenbügel.

Launched in 1924 the Wolkenbügel was a horizontal construction that was to rest on top of three gigantic columns in the centre of Moscow. Lissitzky drew eight of these horizontal skyscrapers around the centre, marking the main roads of the city centre. In 1926 it was laid down that buildings in the city centre were to be limited to six storeys, so the project could not go ahead.

Since then many architects have been inspired by this project, such as the Dutch architect Mart Stam in 1924 and the Japanese Kenzo Tange in 1960. His 'irons of the sky' represented for Lissitzky above all his preoccupation with the new.

The unusual feature of the Wolkenbügel is that the most sought after part of a high-rise building, the top, is used to the full. With today's shortage of land, the Wolkenbügel offers a relatively simple application of a stacked ground level, a strategy that has been cleverly deployed in all its simplicity in the Rotterdam project The Bridge: a 15,000 m² office building that 'floats' above an existing factory complex.

MVRDV,

Housing,

Ypenburg,

design 1999

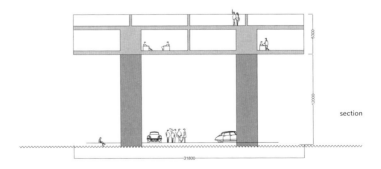

section

Longhouses

Like many other people in the tropics, the Dayak of Borneo and the Papua of New Guinea built their houses on piles. It is a purely functional choice: it makes it harder for snakes and other unpleasant creatures to enter, the houses are safe from flooding during heavy rains, and are easier to defend. These longhouses were built of wood, of course, and were combined to form complete villages. MVRDV drew inspiration from these houses for the raised homes in Ypenburg, though the plans were not implemented.

Iban longhouses,

Borneo

Ontwerpgroep Trude Hooykaas,

Design for Werkgebouw

Kraanspoor,

Amsterdam, 2004

< Art project,

Southern France,

ca. 1974

Alsop Architects,
OCAD Sharp Centre
for Design,
Toronto, 2004

Didden House

In Rotterdam, MVRDV designed a roof landscape for the Didden family on top of a former tram shed. The extension consists of two children's bedrooms and a bedroom for the parents. In the first instance these rooms were set in two double-arched domes separated by a small park, including a picnic table and space to stretch out.

A large number of different constructional methods were investigated for the production of the domes. This exercise was necessary because the architectural ambition proved to be too much for the not inconsiderable budget. The unexpectedly high expenses were partly due to the fact that the original roof construction had to be reinforced. This additional expense (50,000 euro) already swallowed up a large part of the budget. In addition, domes are simply expensive to produce.

The most expensive variant involved applying a layer of insulation and gunned concrete to two custom-made 'bubbles', which would be pricked once the concrete had hardened. Slightly less expensive was the technique of making domes of gunned concrete on wooden formwork. The least expensive was to make the domes with trusses covered with plywood sheeting, insulation material and a layer of polyurethane. This version was still too expensive, and it was not very architecturally satisfying either because the streamlined shapes could not be made with the rigid plywood sheeting. Equally unsatisfactory was the idea of building the domes with aerated cement blocks like igloos and then scraping the outside and the inside into the right shape because the amount of useful space was too small.

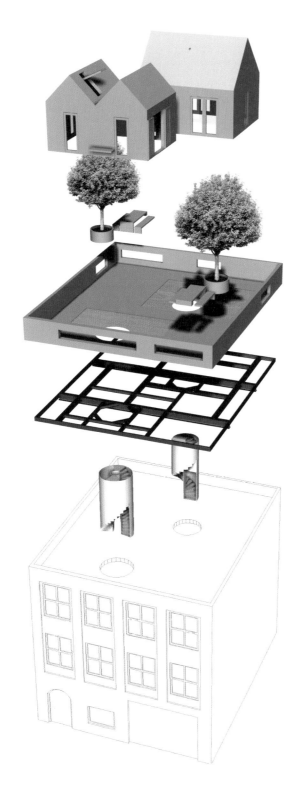

MVRDV,

Design Didden house,

Rotterdam, 2004

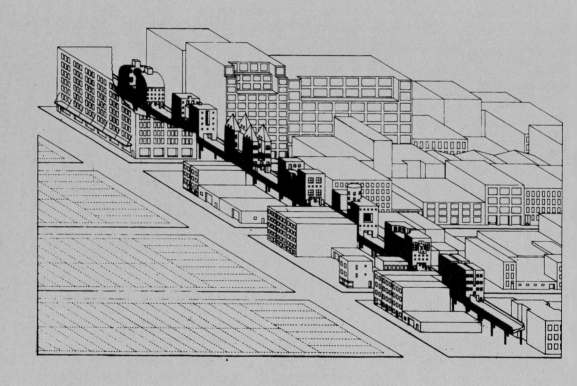

Steven Holl Architects,

Bridge of house,

New York, 1982

Air rights

Air is not free. The air above motorways,
for example, belongs to the Water Board,
the province or the local authority. Dutch Rail
owns the air above the tracks. This makes
building above roads and railway lines
complicated, because the different parties
impose additional demands, which increase the
price. The Water Board, for instance, wants a
guarantee that widening of the roads will still
be possible at any time in spite of the buildings.
Dutch Rail is not exactly dying to sell the air
above its rails either. British Rail is more
progressive in that respect. It sold its rights,
so that it is now possible to build above the
tracks. The best-known project of this kind is
Broadgate, where SOM designed a bridge-like
construction together with a building. British
Rail is using the revenue from the sale of air
rights to renovate the stations. Building in the
air above motorways and railway lines,
however, lies outside the scope of this book.

Skidmore,

Owings & Merrill Inc.,

Design

Broadgate/Liverpool station,

London

Smithfield Village

Smithfield Village is situated north of the centre of Dublin. It is the part where whisky used to be distilled. The architect Andrezej Wejchert has made use of the old, characteristic industrial buildings to transform this entire 30,000 m² area into a new and lively part of the city. The interventions are a mixture of shops, restaurants, exhibition spaces (the Jameson Whisky Centre), a music centre, a hotel, and 224 apartments with roof terraces on the top floors. The smokestack, dating from 1895, has been turned into an observatory tower by placing a glass construction on top of it. A panoramic lift is the spectacular means of access to this tourist attraction.

Building process II

Right from the first moment of human history, ordering, and with it the ordering of the world, has been dominated by the possibility of control. For the last century and a half that control has been linked to the ideology of reproduction. This has strongly reduced diversity in housing.
The attempts of functionalism to translate housing into quantifiable terms were the product of a fascination with the principle of the industrial conveyor belt. The home was divided into purely functional elements that would later be assembled to form a home. In this machine à habiter, each detail was assigned a fixed place in the closed process of production in terms of a functional necessity. But although the housing that emerged from this tradition satisfied a functional programme of requirements, that programme did not satisfy the human demands that can be made of housing.
The problem is that the characteristics of an (old-fashioned) process of production are incompatible with those of a city or a home. The production process must by definition be targeted. After all, the objective is to achieve a result – the production of a particular product, in this case a country's housing – with a minimum of energy. If this is to be done efficiently, the objective must be formulated as precisely as possible. And this is where the problem lies. Housing is an evolving, interactive process, and the functioning of a home must not be allowed to be unambiguous for a single moment. The process of production led to a grim uniformity rather than a flexible and highly differentiated housing environment. This process of production has resulted in homes becoming functionally closed objects that hardly admit of any different interpretations by the occupants (research TU Delft 1992).

< Andrezej Wejchert,

Redevelopment of

Smithfield Village,

Dublin, 1996

Alsop Architects in
collaboration with Jean Nouvel,
Massimiliano Fuksas,
Otto Staadler,
Tower Project Herouville,
France, 1987

Ackermann und Partner,
Märker Zementwerk,
Harburg,
1979

Parking facilities

Every new home in the Netherlands is allocated parking space for one and a half vehicles, as laid down in the Building Regulations. Luxury homes may even have space for two. In itself there is nothing wrong with this measure, since residents in the network city cannot cope without a car. They live a (relatively) long way away from shops, far from school and their place of work, and their leisure is no longer spent in the nearest city, but among a range of cities at home and abroad. A consequence of the planning of new districts, as well as of the Western mentality, is not only that the norm is actually too low (three or four cars are almost normal in a family with adult children), but also that the car has the new housing estates in its clutches. Cars take up a lot of space and go a long way towards determining the look of the street. There are only a few cases where there is enough political and financial elbow-room to design the car out of the picture and to create low-traffic neighbourhoods.

The historic centres already face major parking problems. Parking in the city centre is regarded as an expensive luxury. Increasing the density of these districts would only increase the pressure on the available parking space and push the price up even higher. There is so little room for manoeuvre that even the norm of one and a half parking spaces per home is impossible to achieve. The simplest solution would be to abandon the norm. In that case you would be able to park somewhere in the vicinity (for example, in a nearby car park), but less often right on your doorstep. This is one of the concessions that residents in rooftop buildings will have to make in return for the unique location of their home and/or office. Cities like Amsterdam, however, have carried out interesting studies on an intensification of parking density. Car parks are being designed more intelligently to increase the effective space, and they can be created on smaller and more unusual sites. So-called automatic garages are planned or have already been constructed beneath the canals, beneath squares, and in or beneath monumental buildings. The computer determines where the car is to be parked. The sliding puzzle system is applied to position the car and to manoeuvre it out again. This principle means that only one or two parking spaces in the garage have to be left free.

This conceals cars from sight. The question is whether everyone finds this such an attractive idea. After all, the car is a status symbol. Moreover, especially in the light of the ease with which it is lured to anonymous housing districts, for many people the car – more than their home – is an expression of their personality: you are what you drive. So to tuck the car anonymously away in a car park, however well-organised it may be, seems to go against human nature.

This is part of the brilliance of the urban development plan for the Borneo Sporenburg development in Amsterdam by landscape architect Adriaan Geuze (West 8). He created car-free streets, but instead of hiding cars from sight, the idea was for the residents to park their limousines in their own homes, not just anywhere, but in the most conspicuous place: the ground floor, separated from the street only by a steel fence. The car is literally in the showroom.

Such places will also have to be found for rooftop buildings. Rooftop parking is an obvious choice. It is in line with the logical argument that the roof is no more than a raised ground level on which in theory anything goes. Besides, it saves the surroundings from the problem of density. The car is prominently present in the Best Parking Lot Showroom (1976) by the SITE firm of architects. This design was based not on shopping, but on parking. The parking spaces are pressed together, as it were, creating folds in the road surface. The shops are accommodated in these folds, so that the parked cars become a hanging sign, decoration for the shops. John

Körmeling's proposal for a ferris wheel car park, or the many stacked Smart car parks that have been built, belong to the same category. They make the car a part of the attraction. Bjarne Mastenbroek and Dick van Gameren wanted to rid the public space of the ugly cars in their housing project in Nijmegen. A lift transports the cars to the roof. This has been done before (visitors to the centre of The Hague used to be able to park on the roof of the V&D department store, for instance), but it yields a number of interesting experiences in Nijmegen. For instance, as they walk from their car to their home, the residents can enjoy a fantastic view over the Ooy polders; they can forget the place – the city – for a moment and it becomes fun to go out (for a few moments you imagine you are out in the countryside). In addition, the architects have not got rid of the cars completely. Mastenbroek and Van Gameren have detached the rooftop car park and the concrete supports from the building volume (for architectural reasons, but also to limit the noise from the cars that reaches the apartments below) and allowed it to overhang. In doing so, they make optimal use of the impact that rooftop construction can have. The presence of cars on the roof is just perceptible at street level. While the car forms a part of the (fairground) attraction and its presence is anecdotal in the designs by SITE and Körmeling, in the plan by Mastenbroek and Van Gameren the cars can just peer over the edge, so that they are not entirely removed from sight.

de architectengroep,

Bjarne Mastenbroek and

Dick van Gameren,

Housing Gerard Noodtstraat,

Nijmegen, 1996

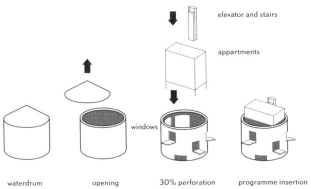

elevator and stairs

appartments

windows

waterdrum   opening   30% perforation   programme insertion

de architectengroep,

Bjarne Mastenbroek and

Dick van Gameren,

Drum house,

Amsterdam, 2000

Noordwestzes architecten,

Renovation of water tower,

Alkmaar, 2002

Scheveningen

The harbour of Scheveningen was originally a fishing port. In the course of time fishery declined in importance and so did the operators. As a result, many old warehouses in the Second Harbour became redundant and are now due for demolition. At the same time, there is a large demand for building land in this area. By renovating the warehouses and placing steel penthouses on their rooftops, the harbour is given a new lease of life.

Archipelontwerpers,

Dokter Lelykade, 1998 and

IJsvis, 1999

Scheveningen

Stepping-stone strategy

The principle on which the stepping-stone strategy is based involves two aspects:
1) the formulation/identification of the theme, and 2) the transformation of the theme. It is
thus not the case that themes are closed systems, like a Lego box, in which the explicit rules of
play have to be taken into account in the search for variants. The reverse is in fact the case.
Because various similarities are introduced into diverse projects, and are also identified as such
at a certain moment, a particular theme emerges as a pattern. This theme then serves as the
starting-point for new variants. All variants also include many non-thematic aspects, variants
and specific solutions, and repetition of these leads to sub-themes. The themes evolve thanks to
these transformations. These aspects of emergence and evolution are the major difference in
approach between Bernard Tschumi's folies for Parc de la Villette in Paris – here the red folies
could be configured precisely on the green grass within the blueprint of strict rules of play –
and the façades that Palladio designed for three churches beside the Canale della Giudecca
in sixteenth-century Venice.
From the Piazza San Marco in Venice you have a good view of the Isola di San Giorgio, where
the famous façade of the San Giorgio Maggiore immediately catches your attention. If you look
further to the right along the Canale della Giudecca, you will be able to distinguish two clearly
proportioned façades among all the heterogeneous buildings of homes and workshops: S. Maria
della Presentazione (Le Zitelle), and Il Redentore.

These two churches combine with San Giorgio
Maggiore to form an architectural front in response
to the open 'urban window' of the Piazza San
Marco. The three façades are not identical, but in
orientation and in composition, colour and material
they have a lot in common.
It was above all Palladio's approach that was
the reference point for Archipelontwerpers in
developing the stepping-stone strategy in
Scheveningen. It was not until after they had
received commissions from two different clients,
followed after a while by a third, to design
penthouses on top of an old warehouse that the
opportunity spontaneously arose of playing a game of references, by which a certain theme was
introduced, though all of this took place without the explicit formulation of
any rules beforehand. So the stepping-stone strategy is a game of
references under construction rather than a developed system within which
certain rules of play have to be followed. Given the specific (technical)
properties of every raised ground level and the at times highly personal
preferences regarding the rooftop home, such tight rules would
be undesirable.

Archipelontwerpers,

De Rokerij,

Scheveningen, 2000

Harbour View

This penthouse designed by Archipelontwerpers, which dates from 1995, was the first step towards rooftop housing. The point of reference for this design was the presence of several robust warehouses with steel cooling plants on the roof. A two-storey, lightweight steel penthouse has been constructed on top of a brick base consisting of two structures that face one another (the plinth) The construction comprises a frame of hot-rolled sections with a lightweight panel filling.

The penthouse was to be used as a home/office and/or studio. These demands were frequently modified and expanded during the building process. The penthouse consists of a single space occupying both storeys. Rooms like the bathroom and bedroom can be partitioned off by means of sliding partitions. The demands were as follows: the residents must be able to look out from the bath over the empty space and see the sea, and once they were out of the bath they must be able to follow different routes through the house.

Essential for this penthouse are the spacious terraces on different levels and the double route afforded by the two staircases.

After the penthouse had been completed, Archipelontwerpers worked on the transformation of a number of warehouses that had been declared obsolete and were due for demolition. Similar steel penthouses are placed on and above these warehouses (IJsvis, Nautilus and Rokerij). The Scheveningen harbour can thus become an example of stepping-stone urban planning.

Archipelontwerpers,

Penthouse Harbour View,

Scheveningen, 1994

'Industrial' design process

There are many names for a multi-layered constellation in which a higher level specifies the scope of decisions taken by the lower level: structure and content, fixed and variable, support and installation, and so on. Such layered structures are to be found not only in architecture but also in art, music, and in a certain sense in all our attempts to classify. Legislation, for instance, makes a distinction between constitutional and regular laws (such as administrative laws, civil codes, etc.). The latter do not have any influence on the constitution, but vice versa the constitution formulates the scope of the other laws.

The rules of a constitution are harder to change than those of the other laws. The constitution could be called relatively fixed, while the other laws are relatively variable.

Seen from this perspective, architecture as an object is not so relevant. What counts in this context is the evaluation of an architectural solution in terms of its capacity, that is, its ability to leave open the possibility of alternative arrangements and programmes. This calls for a different approach to designing housing or buildings in general.

Designing a building of this kind is like formulating a number of rules of play. The idea of generating architecture on the basis of rules of play is implicitly present in the whole history of architecture. From this point of view, the architect targets not the designing of a one-off architectural object, but the processual aspect of housing and working. The architect will have to define the rules of play that determine which situations are possible as in a game of chess: how large a field is, which pieces are operative in it, how they can be grouped, and which moves can be made. In this way the architect can make decisions in a certain situation about the scale, rhythm or repertoire of the elements applied. Each project can thus acquire an identity of its own without design freezing functionality, or vice versa.

Designing is the formulation of the rules of play. Most games, however, have uniform rules that cannot be changed during the game. If we conceive of housing or the city as a game, it is a 'self-changing game', in which the rules can be modified while the game is in progress. We see it as a challenge to consider industrial principles in the light of these evolving rules of play (artificial life).

Rules of play

The idea of generating architecture on the basis of rules of play is not new. It is latent in the earliest theoretical writings on architecture. The rediscovery of the writings of Vitruvius and Palladio's interpretation of them during the Renaissance are particularly relevant in this respect (Scha and Vreedenburgh, 1994). Palladio was the first major architect to base his work (in particular, his designs for villas) on rules of play. He was able to play countless variations on the theme of the villa. A number of Palladio's rules of play can be found in his *I Quattro Libri dell' Architettura* of 1570. Others can be reconstructed through analysis of his villas, as was done by George Hersey and Richard Freedman in 1992. They tested the correctness of their rules by feeding them into a computer and generating algorithmic new designs for Palladian villas on that basis. By using the computer in the analysis of the villas, they were able to make numerous corrections to the studies that have appeared on Palladio in the last four hundred years. Their analysis also showed that Palladio himself did not always apply his rules equally strictly. Palladio's Platonic villa sometimes came to grief in the choice of materials. The rules of play followed by Palladio and his contemporaries were formulated in terms of elementary transformations, such as shifting, rotation and mirror reflection. The same rules were followed for the design of both the parts and the whole. Nature too shows how simple transformational rules can lead to complex systems.

The Hague I

The symposium 'The Hague in search of an extra 2 million square metres of land for housing' was held in 2002. Four speakers indicated how they would find a quarter of the number of square metres required. Eric Vreedenburgh from Archipelontwerpers was commissioned to investigate this, using the rooftop housing approach.
The 500,000 square metres needed are the equivalent of six thousand new homes. To show that this huge number of homes can easily be built on the roofs of The Hague, the following calculation was made, based on the core statistics of The Hague for 2001 and on the land statistics of the Statistics Netherlands for 1996.

Number of homes in The Hague: 215,000
Average surface area: 79 m^2
Total housing surface area: 215,000 x 97 = 16,985,000 m^2

Taking each rooftop home to have an average surface area of about 140 m^2 with a large terrace, the required 500,000 m^2 of surface area for housing is equivalent to 6,329 homes with a surface area of 97 m^2, or 3,600 with a surface area of 140 m^2.

Surface area of The Hague: 8,260 ha
52% is building land: 4,295 ha
37% is building land for housing: 3,056 ha

15% of the houses in The Hague were built before 1910 and are probably less suitable as the base for a rooftop home in structural terms. Of the remaining 85%, about 40% have a flat roof, which is a pre-condition for rooftop construction. This yields 1460.30 ha for building.

A total of 500,000 m^2 of rooftop housing with one-and-a-half storeys requires 334,000 m^2 of rooftop surface level. That is thus 0.8% of the surface area of building land, 1.1% of the surface area of building land for housing, or 2.3% of the available rooftop surface area.

Parks

A large garden has been laid out on the roof of the Chicago City Hall to improve the micro climate. The idea behind it is that the black roofing absorbs and retains heat, which is one of the reasons why the city remains uncomfortably warm for a long time. The city council is therefore encouraging people to create rooftop gardens, and sets a good example itself. It is a pity that the beautifully designed garden with twenty thousand plants is not open to the public. This diminishes the effectiveness of this intervention. Only the users of the neighbouring office blocks can enjoy the greenery. One of the important problems in cities is precisely the lack of greenery, and by turning the roof into a park you make the public space in cities more attractive. Many new building projects all over the world show this.

Conservation Design Forum,

Rooftop garden on

Chicago City Hall,

2001

Archipelontwerpers,

Roof terrace on

former library,

The Hague, 1998

Dovecote, Schilderswijk

The Hague

Uppercity Foundation

Uppercity Foundation is an information network whose aim is to develop and exchange knowledge that is relevant to the development of the urban space above the roof and in the air (see www.bovenstad.nl). It hopes to achieve this objective through research, the exchange of information, and by initiating and supporting a number of projects in the fields of urban renewal, restructuring, renovation and adaptive reuse – that is, urban transformation. Urban transformation is a way of fulfilling the need for spatial planning and housing. The potential of the present-day city must be used to the full, and that calls for an integrated approach: combined improvement of buildings, green space, water, infrastructure and services. Variants such as topping up, the conversion of ground-floor amenities to housing, extension and vertical amalgamation are merely incidents in this process. Those transformations are sought in which the quality of the new adds so much that the existing property also increases in value, especially in use.

Roof terraces in Rome,

Barcelona and Venice

Merle D. McNamee,

Pickup Dormobile,

early 1960

from: *Living in motion*

Ateliers Jean Nouvel,

Design for roof terrace

Les Halles,

Paris, 2004

Meesteren Warehouse

The historic Meesteren Warehouse building in Rotterdam is situated in the new district called Kop van Zuid. This is the location where the development of Rotterdam harbour got under way more than a century ago. The Meesteren Warehouse was built in the 1940s, and was later topped up with an extra storey. In the early plans for Kop van Zuid this warehouse was considered obsolete and ripe for demolition. The Japanese architect Fumi Hoshino was commissioned by Van Ginneken Vastgoed to draw up a plan to give the warehouse a second life with a new function. An important part of this transformation consists of adding twenty-one rooftop penthouses.

To make optimal use of the limited space, to retain the historic character of the warehouse, and to achieve a maximum of privacy for the penthouses, it was decided to cut through the building diagonally along the city's East-West visual axis. By making the diagonal with two different angles (30 and 60 degrees), optimal use was made of the sunlight. The dark building was opened up in a few places.

The existing warehouse doors have been turned to face outwards on every floor. The historic façades remain more or less intact. Where possible, and within certain limits, they are even being allowed to continue to decay.

Because of the additional weight of the penthouses, the building had to be given a new concrete foundation to replace the wooden pile construction. This wooden foundation was originally intended for a one-floor warehouse; through the addition of extra layers, the moment came when its maximum capacity had been reached. The creation of a new foundation also made it possible to include parking facilities beneath the warehouse.

The ground floor of the building is reserved for shops and catering establishments, with two floors of offices above them. The original roof will accommodate gardens, a tea-house, and the apartments.

These 21 penthouses vary in size from 100 to 300 m², and are situated behind the extended diagonal 60-degree axis. They are distributed over several storeys and a lift connects the private area directly with the basement garage. Visitors can ring the bell outside the building and take the garden lift upstairs, which brings them to the garden that has been laid out on the present roof level. The building administration system guides them from there along a short path to the general entrance of the apartments.

Fumi Hoshino,

Design for penthouses

Meesteren Warehouse,

Rotterdam, 1999

LOT/EK Ada Tolla and
Giuseppe Lignano,
Guzman Penthouse,
New York, 1996

Covered roof terrace

Han Slawik has designed a glass-covered terrace for the top-most apartment of a five-storey building in the centre of Amsterdam. The glass roof consists of a Rondogard construction of wood and acrylic glass. Unlike ordinary glass, the sheets of acrylic glass allow 80 per cent of UV rays to pass through, thereby allowing the residents to tan naturally. Because of the wind and rain, roof terraces can only be used for an average of three to six weeks a year in the Netherlands. This covering enables the owners to use the roof terrace for a much longer period.

The quarter-circle one-metre thick segments are made of a glued construction of (laminated) wooden trusses with two sliding parts. Each segment weighs no more than 40 kg, including the panes of glass. The main supporting construction consists of a rigid steel frame that transfers the forces through an edge beam to a new floor. This floor is composed of a layer of timber beams covered with profiled metal sheets with 60 mm concrete. The floor is finished with slabs of Carrara marble. It is preferable to terracotta slabs because although the thermal storage capacity of terracotta from solar radiation would have been welcome in the spring and the autumn, it would have been unbearable in the summer.

Han Slawik,

Covered roof terrace,

Amsterdam, 1991

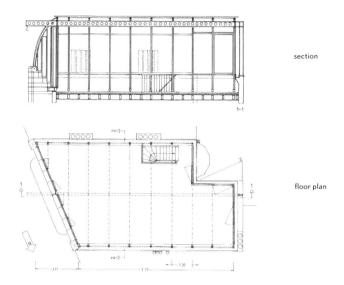

section

1-1

floor plan

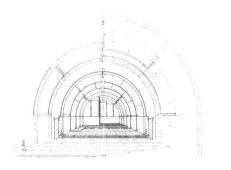

axonometric projection

Durability

The approach to durability practised in the building
industry usually leads to regulations and discussions about the
degree of insulation and the materials that are to be used.
Although there is no doubt about the value of these aspects,
durable building includes facets that have not received much
attention so far. Durability must above all be a
mentality that is by definition not bound by scale and that
transcends the many boundaries that are erected in the
Netherlands between all kinds of disciplines with their many
subsidiary interests. Many new housing estates have been built
during the last few decades or are under construction today.

These plans have to comply with standards for durable
building in most local districts; some neighbourhoods go even
further and build in an ecological manner. All the same, it is
debatable whether these new housing estates really really do
make for a more durable use of land. For example, most homes
have such a rigid interior arrangement that they are only suitable for a standard middle-class family consisting of a father, a
mother, two children and a dog. When there is no longer
demand for this type of home, it is practically impossible to
incorporate other functions into it, so its actual durability is
very limited. Moreover, these estates usurp large tracts of the
country because of their relatively low building density, even
though there is an enormous potential in the cities which is
hardly used, if at all. One alternative to the exodus from the
city to the Vinex housing estate is rooftop housing.

We interpret durability as making use of the full potential of
what has already been provided (built). For instance, what we
know is based on rethinking and interpreting the knowledge
that has been accumulated by earlier generations. Many cities
are built on sites previously occupied by primitive settlements
and those settlements came into being at the spot where two
trade routes intersected. Seen in this light, we are surprised at
the clumsy and uncreative way that cities are used.

The Hague II

The report *Extra bouwlaag* [Extra storey] was issued in The Hague at the beginning of 2004 as part of the Architectural Advisory Report. This policy ties in with the local authority's plan for the development of a part of the city. It must provide space for expanding the surface area of the city used for housing as well as criteria for the quality of that expansion. Rooftop buildings, according to this report, are never isolated. They always form part of the street wall and are often one of several rooftop buildings which combine to form an extra storey on top of a block of buildings.

The aim of this local authority report is twofold. It calls for a lack of ambiguity to ensure the quality of the individual building plans and an overall quality for larger numbers of rooftop buildings.

The policy indicates which steps are required in the design process in order to arrive at the concept of rooftop construction. The relationship with the existing architecture is an important principle, according to the same report. On the basis of a plan in stages, the architect can design the rooftop building and the architectural advisory committee can evaluate the plan.

Stage 1: The question of whether an extra storey can be built or not is determined by urban planning frameworks such as the zoning plan. Moreover, there are situations which make an extra storey impossible: the existing roof may not be structurally suitable, or the building may be an architectural monument.

Stage 2: This is the stage in which it is decided whether the rooftop building is to have an individual impact or whether it forms part of an architectural ensemble with a high level of unity. This consideration is connected with the degree of variation in the district or street.

Stage 3: Three methods can be distinguished when it comes to adding an extra storey. According to the report, these are: a) designing to fit in with the existing architecture; b) designing to contrast with the existing architecture; or c) designing a corrective rooftop building, which entails a structural refit of the premises beneath it and thus an upgrading of the existing architecture.

Penthousing

The Rotterdam local authority is launching initiatives aimed at promoting the building of new homes on existing premises under the name 'penthousing'. It interprets penthousing as the addition of one or two extra homes to a building. The local authority wants more people to live in the centre of the city and greater differentiation in housing. It intends to realise this objective by using not only the top storeys of new building complexes, but also the roofs of existing buildings. To widen the range of options, penthouses and other buildings will be built. The local authority is making special subsidies available to encourage this development.

Penthouses, in the vision of the local authority, are not only effective in connection with the intensive use of space, but can also give the host premises a genuine facelift, as well as helping to improve the the city's overall appearance. Rotterdam already has a reputation as an architecture city, and that image will only be strengthened, the local authority believes, if attractive rooftop buildings are built. The centre is particularly interesting in this connection, but there are plenty of possibilities outside the centre as well.

The Rotterdam local authority states that in principle penthousing is permitted everywhere, unless a current zoning plan or monument status clearly rules it out. Otherwise, the following criteria apply:

1) The host building must benefit from the addition because its image is improved, a lift is added, or other improvements are made to the building.

2) The additions must tie in with the host building. This does not necessarily mean more of the same. The image (architecture) may be different and challenging, as long as there is evident respect for the host building and the surroundings. The architectural advisory committee advises on this.

3) Although the local authority would prefer to see the joint provision of every building in a block with new penthouses, that is not necessary, though the local authority will encourage this in the future. (Rotterdam local authority brochure, 2004.)

Costs

Amsterdam discovered the advantage of extra storeys in the mid-1990s. Extra subsidies were made available to intensify the use of space through topping up and to improve the quality of the built environment. Three projects – IJsdoornlaan (North Amsterdam), Complex 50 (Osdorp) and Complex 24 (Geuzenveld) – were subsequently evaluated to determine whether topping up really was an effective form of urban enhancement and whether it was financially feasible in all cases.

In retrospect, the fact that the topping up of Complex 24 was called off during the investigatory stage anticipated the conclusions of the report. Topping up is expensive and thus more expensive than standard new building. According to the researchers, this is connected with the long planning stage and the high consultancy fees. The contract price also turned out to be much higher than the cost of building houses on a new housing estate. This was due to the fact that the homes were not very deep and to the costs of the extension and covering of the ventilation and chimney flues from the building below, the constructional attachments to the existing block and the conditions for them imposed by the architectural advisory committee, the extra costs entailed by a lighter building method, the extra expenses entailed by the fact that the building activities were carried out on the roof, an expensive staircase, and a large area of the façade that was transparent.

The most obvious but most superficial conclusion might be that demolition and starting anew is financially more attractive than topping up and restoration. There are other arguments too, the report states, such as housing differentiation, parking solutions, and substantial improvements to the public space, which are in favour of demolition and rebuilding. Adding layers, the report concludes, is only interesting for complexes with a certain future value.

At the same time, these are arguments in favour of rooftop housing as opposed to topping up. Topping up is based on the same lack of ambition as council housing or Vinex estates. It all has to be done on the cheap, so the yield is minimal. In fact, nothing really changes at all – the building just gains one storey, or at most two.

Rooftop construction, on the other hand, is highly ambitious, particularly in the West, where the more expensive penthouses are rooftop buildings. This is the only way to achieve social, economic, architectural and urban developmental differentiation. The remark that adding layers is only interesting for complexes with a certain future value applies primarily to topping up, because in many cases these extensions have little or no impact of their own, but it overlooks the impact of rooftop construction, a building process that enhances the building not only in terms of architecture or urban development, but also economically.

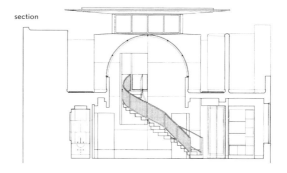

section

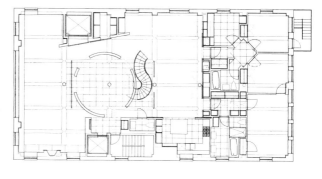

floor plan

Shelton, Mindel & Associates,

Manhattan Penthouse,

New York, 1998

Deck House

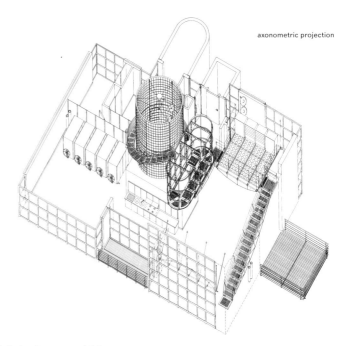

This penthouse – the Deck House – was designed at the same time as the apartment complex beneath it. Most of the volume of the penthouse is situated within the envelope of the new building. Only the bathroom appears as an autonomous volume above the roof. This circular bathroom tower consists of a steel frame filled with translucent glass bricks. The roof is made of transparent glass.

The lift leads to the extra high bathroom, which affords an impressive view of the river. An open steel stairway leads up to a hanging steel platform that functions as a bedroom. With an incredible sensitivity to refinement and craftsmanship, the penthouse refers in space, material and detail to the original industrial character of this setting. It turns a very optimistic back on a traditional domestic lifestyle.

Richard Rogers,

Deck House,

London, 1989

floor plan

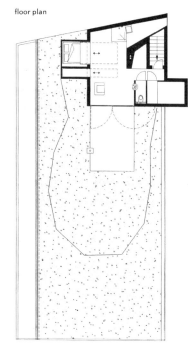

Pool Architektur,

T.O. Penthouse,

Vienna, 2000

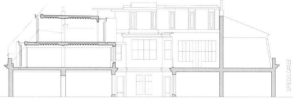

section

Rudiger Lainer,

Penthouse, Seilergasse,

Vienna, 1991

Archipelontwerpers with
Wim van de Kamer,
Penthouse Rokin,
Amsterdam, 2000

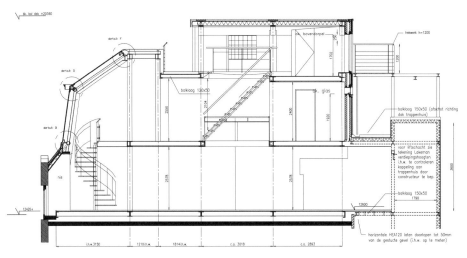

section

Holzbox Tirol (Armin Kathan),

    MiniBox,

Innsbruck, 1999

Andreas Hild and
Tillman Kaltwasser,
Bonnin House,
Eichstätt, 1995

IFD

Buildings that are designed and constructed according to the principles of Industrial Flexible and Dismountable (IFD) must satisfy the demands of the occupier, provide better working conditions in the construction industry, and lead to improved cooperation and harmonisation between all of the parties involved in the building process. Their flexibility gives the buildings a longer shelf-life, and the prefabrication results in a higher degree of perfection than traditional building techniques offer.

In themselves, these objectives are clearly identifiable. The most important point, however, is that these building systems too focus exclusively on designing homes. The questions that then arise are: How effective is the home, and what is its relation to industrial building?

The attempts of functionalism to conceive of housing in quantifiable terms arose from a fascination with the principle of the conveyor belt. The home was to become a machine à habiter, in which every detail acquires a fixed place in the closed process of production based on a functional necessity.

The objective of a process of production is to manufacture a particular product – in this case a home or housing environment – with a minimum of energy. If this is to be done efficiently, the objective must be formulated as precisely as possible. This is where the elusive element of this trajectory lies. Housing cannot be defined in language. Housing is open to many interpretations, it reflects cultures and subcultures, and is bound to a certain period. It seems to live a life of its own, a life that cannot be domesticated and predicted by matrices, scenarios or visual reference plans.

It can be claimed that the housing which was the product of this modernist tradition satisfied a functional programme of demands, but that this programme in itself did not function, nor did it satisfy the (existential) demands that can be made of housing.

That is why it is important to search for other strategies of industrial building – not strategies that are geared to the production of monocultures, but strategies with flexibility, interaction and individual choice as ingredients. In the world of 'the genuine industrially manufactured product' such as the automotive or electronics industries, where mass production has been replaced by lean production (smaller series, much variety, and just-in-time), this approach is completely normal by now. The production of architecture, however, is still trapped in the prewar idiom of neutral reproducibility.

Flexibility is becoming a trendy term in building at the moment. Flexibility, however, is not an objective in itself, but a possible answer to the question of how much mental room for manoeuvre you want to give people to live in – a notion that is becoming increasingly individual and differentiated as a result of various social trends. It refers to an interaction between occupier and home. Flexibility is not intended to drive people into a mobilised and technological landscape, but to let people settle down in dialogue with their home environment. It is precisely neutral – so-called functional – housing that turns people into strangers in their own homes. Flexibility in the building process is merely a first reply to the question of how architecture can anticipate diversity and change.

Diversity is connected with a reflection of individual preferences in a pluriform society at a particular moment in time, while change emphasises the temporal aspect of this issue.

Nature shows that everything is subject to the ravages of time. Change also means letting go, and thus uncertainty. And that is something which our technology has great problems in facing.

Archipelontwerpers,

Design for 5 penthouses,

Maasstraat,

Rotterdam, 2000

Archipelontwerpers,

Design for penthouse,

Grote Marktstraat,

The Hague, 2000

Design

Although architecture and urban development have never been so much discussed as in the last century, nor had so much been 'deliberately' planned before then, the developments in our cities have never been as unpredictable and uncontrollable as they are today. What is so striking is the massive discrepancy between ideal and reality. The discussion of how design has lost its effectiveness is derived from our changed attitude to what we call design. A design is intended to arrange certain things, but at the same time it is itself a part of that arrangement. In that sense, our views on urban development and architecture are very accurate reflections of shifts in how we think.

Heterarchy

Concepts, organisations, homes and other constellations derive their significance from the relations between the different elements. These relations are growing increasingly complex.

Our observations are also a part of that network of relations, and are therefore by no means neutral. We try to create perspectives from arbitrary positions in that network, situated in both time and space. We see them as hierarchical arrangements in which all the elements are in a certain order, which we can perceive. But each element can also participate in the other orders. Thus what a house means for its occupant is not the same as what it means for the developer, architect, postman or burglar. So a tree structure can be set up from every element, such as the home. However, many tree structures deriving from an equal number of layers of meaning can be super imposed in the home. And although each tree structure displays one-dimensional characteristics, the path through these structures can be followed in a variety of ways. New paths with new layers of meaning are being created all the time. This activity leads to a growing complexity, whose unpredictability increases the further you go.

From an arbitrary position, we try to catch the world, or a city, within a hierarchical structure of perception, but if we change our position, the perspective changes, and with it the hierarchy.

The different perspectives that one can see from a particular position form the meaning of that position. They are literal intersections within a specific time-space. Simultaneously participating in the different hierarchies yields the picture of a heterarchy. The complexity and concomitant proliferation in a city constitute an appropriate example of a heteropolis.

Cities, software programs and business organisations are composed of several layers of elements and processes that are simple in themselves. However, these elements do not exist in isolation, but influence one another.

The result is a complexity that can no longer be comprehended by designers and administrators. The analytical, purposive way we organise and design seems to backfire on us. This is because it is quite impossible to explicitly specify the functioning of a city, a home or an organisation. This can only be done in dialogue with the users, and it can change over the course of time too. There is no reason why the functioning of a city like that will be unambiguously fixed for a single moment (Vreedenburgh, 1998).

Ever since the rise of humanism, design, including the arrangement of the world, has been dominated by the possibility of control. This fact, linked to the ideology of reproducibility, has sharply reduced diversity in housing over the last hundred and fifty years. Functional analyses of a design plan led to general and therefore impersonal solutions in housing.

Restoration Mies' penthouse

This two-storey penthouse was designed by Ludwig Mies van der Rohe in 1956 on top of the roof of a tower apartment block in Chicago. One of the later owners added walls and rooms, resulting in an unfortunate disruption of the original spatial concept. The Powell/Kleinschmidt architectural duo restored the penthouse in 2001 for the present owner, thereby rescuing Mies' original design.

Powell/Kleinschmidt,

Restoration Mies' Penthouse,

1956, Chicago,

1992

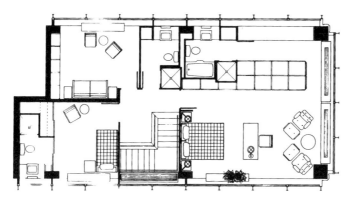

second floor

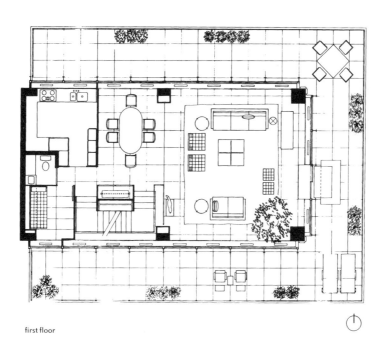

first floor

Hoogstad Architecten,

Penthouse Westerkade,

Rotterdam, 1999

Penthouse Rotterdam

The home that Jan Hoogstad designed for himself beside the River Maas in Rotterdam is a classic example of a penthouse that affords a relaxed but metropolitan lifestyle. The penthouse is situated on top of a five-storey office block. The top floor has been opened up and transformed into a living room and spacious roof terrace. A second housing layer has been laid on top of the existing concrete construction. The 'ground' floor of this two-storey home consists of a hall, kitchen and living room. The second floor contains a bedroom, study, bathroom and wardrobe. The living room is divided into a low section with an intimate character – including an open hearth – and a section twice as high penetrated on all four sides by daylight that enters through large glass partitions with wooden shutters on the outside.

Implants

Rooftop construction also provides a new strategy for new building. Placing buildings on top of one another leads to programmatic differentiation and architectural diversity. The dissonance that the difference in styles produces is a challenge to deal less rigidly with new buildings than when everything is designed by the same architect. The different styles also entail a layeredness of scale, allowing these buildings to become more organically embedded in an urban context. A well-known example of this strategy is the new building of the Groningen Museum. The basic design from 1988-1994 is by the Italian architect Alessandro Mendini. In his concept, the museum is divided up into different pavilions. Guest architects were invited to complete the designing of several of these pavilions. There are two pavilions, one stacked on top of the other, on the west side of the museum. The lower pavilion is for the archaeology and history of the city and province of Groningen. It was designed by the Italian designer Michelle de Lucchi in red brick. On top of it is a circular pavilion designed by the French designer Philippe Starck. This volume clad with large aluminium plates accommodates the applied art collection.

At the other end of the museum, on the roof, is the most autonomous pavilion. The open volume, designed by the Viennese firm of architects Coop Himmelb(l)au, is composed of double-sided steel plate alternating with tempered glass, and is used for temporary exhibitions. This collection of pavilions forms a collage of spaces, programmes and materials with a diversity of character that one rarely comes across in new building projects.

A large apartment block that was recently built in IJburg is similar in process, though the programme and elaboration are completely different.

Several architects had to work together on one block for this new district of Amsterdam. Block 16A was designed by Vera Yanovshtchinsky Architecten together with Archipelontwerpers. Instead of dividing the block into a number of plots to be designed by the two architects, it was decided that Vera Yanovshtchinsky Architecten would design a total structure within which Archipelontwerpers would introduce a number of implants, based on a few simple agreements regarding construction, access, cabling and piping, and materials. Two of the steel implants explicitly refer – as a statement – to the Harbour View penthouse in Scheveningen.

Yanovshtchinsky Architecten

in collaboration

with Archipelontwerpers,

Implant housing IJburg,

Amsterdam, 2000

Index of satellite texts

Literature

Literature consulted

Apollinaire, G. (1910), *L'hérésiarque et Cie.* Paris: Stock. (English translation 2004, *The Heresiarch & Co.* Cambridge, Mass.: Exact Change).

Baudrillard, J. (2000), *The Vital Illusion.* New York: Columbia University Press.

Castells, M. (1996; 2000). *The Rise of the Network Society.* Oxford: Blackwell.

CIAM (1933). Charter of Athens. 'Die Functionelle Stadt', pamphlet, 1933 (published in :*Weiterbauen* 1934, 1-2, Annales Techniques (1933), 44-46).

Debord, G. (1967). *La société du spectacle.* Paris: Buchet Chastel. (English translation 1995 *The Society of the Spectacle,* Cambridge, Mass.: MIT Press).

ds+V, Housing department (January 2004), Brochure *Penthousing in Rotterdam.* Rotterdam: Rotterdam Local Authority.

Friedman, Y. (1956). L' Architecture Mobile'. In: Yona Friedman (1999). *Structures Serving the Unpredictable.* Rotterdam: NAi Publishers.

Gausa, M. (1998). *Housing: New Alternatives, New Systems.* Boston: Birkhauser.

Go, F., Klooster, E. van 't, Fenema, P.C. van, and Jager, W.P. de (2003). *Wereldspeler van formaat: op weg naar de Deltametropool.* The Hague: SMO.

Hersey, G. and Freedman, R. (1992). *Possible Palladian Villas (Plus a Few Instructively Impossible Ones).* Cambridge, Mass.: MIT Press.

Jarry, A. (1911). *Gestes et opinions du docteur Faustroll, pataphysicien.* (English translation 1996 *Exploits And Opinions Of Dr. Faustroll, Pataphysician: A Neo-Scientific Novel,* Cambridge, Mass.: Exact Change).

Kelk, F. (1974). Constant: 'Mijn antithese tot de leugenmaatschappij'. In: *Elseviers Weekblad,* 6 July 1974.

Koolhaas, R. (1995). 'Generic City' (essay). Sassenheim: Sikkens Foundation. Previously published in: *S, M, L, XL: Office for Metropolitan Architecture.* Rotterdam: 010; New York: Monacelli Press, 1995.

LeWitt, S. (1969). 'Sentences on conceptual art'. In: *Art Language 1,* 1 May 1969.

Lissitzky-Küppers, S. (1967). *El Lissitzky. Maler, Architekt Typograf, Fotograf: Erinnerungen, Briefe, Schriften.* Dresden: Verlag der Kunst. (English translation 1978 *El Lissitzky. Life, Letters, Texts,* London: Thames & Hudson).

Locher, J.L. (1974). *New Babylon.* The Hague: Haags Gemeentemuseum.

Melet, E. (1997). 'Symbiotisch penthouse'. In: *De Architect* 4, April 1997, The Hague: ten Hagen & Stam.

Palladio, A. (1570). *I Quattro Libri dell' Architettura.* Facsimile reprint 1949, Milan: Hoepli.

Scha, R. and Vreedenburgh, E. (1994). 'Vers une autre Architecture'. In: *Zeezucht 8,* The Hague: Theater Zeebelt.

Scha, R. (1991). 'Artificiële Kunst'. In: *Zeezucht 4,* The Hague: Theater Zeebelt.

Sorkin, M. (ed.) (1992). *Variations on a Theme Park. The New American City and the End of Public Space.* New York: Hill & Wang.

Vierde Nota Ruimtelijke Ordening Extra (1990). The Hague: VROM.

Vreedenburgh, E. (1992). *Bouwproduktontwikkeling: ontwikkelingen voorbij het produkt.* Delft: Technical University Delft.

Vreedenburgh, E. (1998). 'De intelligente stad'. In: *De onvermijdelijke culturele revolutie.* The Hague: SMO.

Wisse, J.F.N. and Bosma, T. (2004). *Welstandsnota Den Haag.* The Hague: DSO The Hague Local Authority.

www.bovenstad.nl

Recommended literature

Asseldonk, T. van, Berger, L. and Hartigh, E. den (2002). *Complexiteit van Alledag.* Zeist: Uitgeverij Kerckebosch.

Heidegger, M. (1954). *Vorträge und Aufsätze.* Pfullingen: Verlag Gunther Neske. (English translation 1975 'Building Dwelling Thinking'. In: *Poetry, Language, Thought,* New York: Harper & Row.).

Heynen, H. (1999). *Architecture and Modernity. A critique.* Cambridge, Mass.: MIT Press.

Wigley, M. (1998). *Constant's New Babylon. The Hyper-Architecture of Desire.* Rotterdam: 010.

The authors

Ed Melet is a freelance writer and lecturer. After graduating as an architect in 1992, he worked for seven years for the periodical *de Architect*. His articles focus primarily on the integration of engineering in architecture. His books include *Sustainable Architecture* (1999) and *The Architectural Detail* (2002). He lectures at the Hogeschool van Amsterdam and the Academy of Architecture in Tilburg.

Eric Vreedenburgh is an architect. After graduating from the Technical University Delft, he set up the Archipel Ontwerpers firm of architects in 1984. He was associated on a part-time basis with the Image and Sound Interfaculty of the Royal Conservatory in The Hague and conducted research at the TU Delft for several years on product development and flexibility. He teaches part-time at the Royal Academy of Fine Art. He has cooperated with various partners to design a number of rooftop buildings.

Photo credits

Heimo Aga: p. 175

Rogier Alleblas: p. 155 b

Alsop Architects: p. 146

Archipelontwerpers: p. 56, 57, 132 b, 152, 153, 160, 166-168, 188-189

Architect Manuel Herz: p. 112

Archives d'Architecture Moderne, Brussel: p. 42

Archivio Superstudio, Florence: p. 6

Yann Artus-Bertrand / Altitude: p. 60

Atelier Jean Nouvel, Artefactory: p. 58-59

Atelier Jean Nouvel, AJN: p. 165

Bias Architecten bv: p. 128

Tom Bonner: p. 119

Anne Bousema: p. 75, 77

Santiago Cirugeda Parejo: p. 100

Conservation Design Forum Inc. Elmhurst, Illinois, Mark Farina, Chicago DOE: p. 159

Peter Cox: p. 79

Luc Deleu (SABAM): p. 132 o

Stefan Eberstadt, Rocket Gallery, London: p. 96

Gerda Eichholzer: p. 186

George Fessy: p. 110, 111

Yona Friedman: p. 52

Christian Gahl: p. 37 l, o

Collection Gemeentemuseum Den Haag: p. 44, 46

Kurt Handlbauer: p. 62, 65

Rob 't Hart: p. 69, 131

Michael Heinrich: p. 187

Sjaak Henselmans: p. 196-197

Hollandia B.V., Nieuwerkerk a/d IJssel: p. 129

Hertha Hurnaus: p. 182

Steffen Jänicke: p. 80

Richard Johnstone: p. 138-139

Nicholas Kane: p. 150

Faz Keuzenkamp: p. 194, 195

Ian Knaggs, p. 108, 109

John Körmeling: p. 72

Hans van Leeuwen: p. 64 b

Lingotto: p. 103

Luxcrete, London: p. 180, 181

Jon Miller © Hedrich Blessing: p. 192

Michael Moran: p. 178, 179

MVRDV: p. 51, 54, 71, 73, 134

Hans Neudecker: p. 147

NL Architects: p. 64

Office for Metropolitan Architecture, Rotterdam: p. 115, 116

Annika en Hakan Olsson: p. 98, 99

Rpbw, Renzo Piano Building Workshop, Berengo Gardin Gianni: p. 104

Rpbw, Renzo Piano Building Workshop, Denancé Michel: p. 105

Rpbw, Renzo Piano Building Workshop, Cano Enrico: p. 107

Courtesy Michael Rakowitz: p. 92

Christian Richters: p. 120-123, 148

Richard Rogers Partnership: p. 94, 95

Han Slawik: p. 172, 173

Margherita Spiluttini: p. 183

David Stansbury Photography, Springfield MA: p. 38

Ron Tetteroo: p. 154, 155 o, 184, 185

Olaf Tompot: p. 135

The architects Skidmore, Owings & Merrill Inc.: p. 143

Elly Valkering: p. 151

Collection Van Abbemuseum, Eindhoven: p. 133

Alberto Venzago / Nacasa & Partners Inc.: p. 91

Marieke Vijfwinkel: p. 12

Eric Vreedenburgh: p. 34-37, 97, 101, 102, 113, 136, 144, 145, 156, 157, 161-163, 200, 201

Paul Warchol: p. 170, 171

Gert Winkler: p. 88

Ingenieursbureau Zonneveld bv.: Rotterdam, p. 128 ro

Gerald Zugmann: p. 125-127

Kim Zwarts: p. 64 o

from: Charles Jencks, The Language of Post-Modern Architecture, Londen: Academy Editions: p. 14

from: Sophie Lissitzky-Küppers, El Lissitzky, Londen: Thames and Hudson: p. 50

from: GA Architect 11, Steven Holl, Tokio: A.D.A. Edita: p. 142

from: Dr. Robert Kronenburg, Living in motion; Design and Architecture for Flexible Dwelling, Weil am Rhein: Vitra Design Museum: p. 164

from: John M. Johansen, Nanoarchitecture A New Species of Architecture, New York: Princeton Architectural Press: p. 55

from: SITE, Highrise of Homes, New York: Rizzoli: p. 67, p. 69 b, 70

This publication was made possible through the financial support of

Netherlands Architecture Fund

IPSV/IFD

Dura Vermeer, Rotterdam

Stichting Habiforum, Gouda

Concept and text   Ed Melet and Eric Vreedenburgh

English translation   Peter Mason

Text editing   Robyn de Jong-Dalziel

Image editing   the authors in collaboration with Janine Schulze

Graphic design   Rick Vermeulen, Natascha Frensch / Via Vermeulen

Printing   Die Keure, Bruges

Paper   Eurobulk, 135 grs.

Binding   Catherine Press, Bruges

Production   Barbera van Kooij, NAi Publishers

Publisher   Simon Franke, NAi Publishers

The authors wish to thank

Luit de Haas / Rob Heilbron / Johan Hofman / Cees Hogervorst / Rob van Hoogdalem / Dick de Jong /
Gert Middelkoop / Marco Pastors / Henk Prins / Maarten Schmitt / Cilian Terwindt /Martin Verwoest /
Rob Vester / Piet Vollaard

For works of visual artists affiliated with a CISAC-organization the copyrights have been settled with Beeldrecht in Amsterdam. © 2005, c/o Beeldrecht Amsterdam

NAi Publishers is an internationally orientated publisher specialized in developing, producing and distributing books on architecture, visual arts and related disciplines.
www.naipublishers.nl info@naipublishers.nl

Although every effort was made to find the copyright holders for the illustrations used, it has not been possible to trace them all. Interested parties are requested to contact NAi Publishers, Mauritsweg 23, 3012 JR Rotterdam, The Netherlands.

Available in North, South and Central America through D.A.P./Distributed Art Publishers Inc, 155 Sixth Avenue 2nd Floor, New York, NY 10013-1507, Tel 212 6271999, Fax 212 6279484.

Available in the United Kingdom and Ireland through Art Data, 12 Bell Industrial Estate, 50 Cunnington Street, London W4 5HB, Tel 208 7471061, Fax 208 7422319.

Printed and bound in Belgium.

ISBN 90-5662-363-X

Cover:

Annika and Hakan Olsson,

Penthouse Albert Court,

London,

2000